THE
DINOSAUR
DELUSION

DISMANTLING EVOLUTION'S MOST CHERISHED ICON

ERIC LYONS AND KYLE BUTT

APOLOGETICS PRESS

APOLOGETICS PRESS, INC.

230 LANDMARK DRIVE

MONTGOMERY, ALABAMA 36117

COPYRIGHT 2008

SECOND PRINTING 2011

ISBN: 978-1-60063-010-1

PRINTED IN CHINA

LAYOUT AND DESIGN BY ROB BAKER

SPECIAL THANKS TO LEWIS LAVOIE (WWW.LAVOIESTUDIOS.COM), DON PATTON, AND BIBLE.CA, FOR PERMISSION TO USE SEVERAL OF THEIR ILLUSTRATIONS AND PICTURES IN THIS BOOK.

Library of Congress Cataloging-in-Publication

Eric Lyons (1975 -) and Kyle Butt (1976 -)

The Dinosaur Delusion

Includes bibliographic references

ISBN-10: 1-60063-010-3

ISBN-13: 978-1-60063-010-1

1. Creation. 2. Science and religion. 3. Apologetics and polemics I. Title

213—dc22   2008931971

DEDICATION

To the staff of Apologetics Press. We thank you for your friendship, your godly lives, and your tireless efforts to produce and disseminate eternally beneficial materials. May God continue to bless you and your families.

Contents

PREFACE

Some time ago, in a small rural church in Tennessee, a teacher asked the adult ladies Bible class what they knew about dinosaurs. The 13 ladies in the class explained that the previous preacher at the congregation taught that dinosaurs never existed. They simply were a figment of the scientific mind, fraudulently concocted to promote evolution.

This is not the first time we have heard of Christians being taught that dinosaurs never existed. In fact, in our travels, numerous people, after listening to our lectures on dinosaurs, have approached us explaining that they were taught that dinosaurs never really lived. These people are the mothers and fathers, grandmothers and grandfathers of the current generation of children in the Church.

What happens when a child learns about dinosaurs at school, comes home to mom and dad with questions, and is informed that dinosaurs never existed? As that child matures, sees the abundant fossil evidence, and visits various museums chock-full of dinosaur remains, his confidence in his parents' ideas about dinosaurs begins to erode. Not only does he begin to question his parents' teachings about the existence of dinosaurs, but he has been set up to be the perfect target for the mass of false evolutionary propaganda strapped to the subject of dinosaurs.

The topic of dinosaurs is something that children are going to learn–from someone! Whether it is from us, or from the evolutionists, children will learn about these creatures. It is interesting, during lectures on dinosaurs, to have a little contest between the people in attendance. The team division is simple: all the kids are on one team and all the adults are on the other. Then, several dinosaur pictures flash onto the screen and the teams are asked to identify the types of dinosaurs in the pictures. *Triceratops, Stegosaurus, Oviraptor,* and *Styracosaurus* are among the group. Which team, adults or kids, do you think correctly identifies the most dinosaurs? Of course you probably know that kids beat the adults almost every time. In fact, most of the adults have no idea which dinosaurs are which, and they certainly cannot accurately pronounce the polysyllabic names the scientific community uses to identify the dinosaurs. But the kids can. What does that say about the information regarding dinosaurs that our children have? Where are they getting it? Or, maybe a better question would be, where are they **not** getting it? Generally speaking, it is **not** coming from their parents, grandparents, preachers, or Bible teachers. Rather, it is coming from an atheistic scientific community that wants to eradicate your child's faith in God.

Due to dinosaurs' iconic evolutionary status, those who believe in God and His Word should be sufficiently informed

about dinosaurs in order to answer the difficult questions that swirl around these creatures. This book is not an exhaustive treatment of dinosaurs. You will not find lists of dinosaur names, or learn how fast *T. rex* might have run, or discover the secrets of restructuring the bones of *Argentinosaurus*, etc. But you will learn about the most pertinent issues in the dinosaur discussion, as that discussion relates to the creation/evolution debate. In the following pages, you will be equipped with the evidence that indicates dinosaurs and humans lived together, and see how dinosaurs fit perfectly into a straightforward reading of the biblical account of Creation.

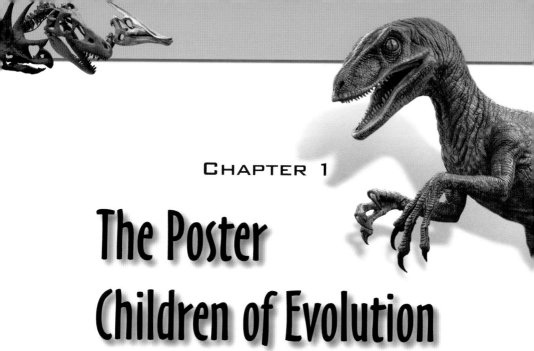

CHAPTER 1

The Poster Children of Evolution

No animal, extinct or living, captures the attention of mankind more than dinosaurs. For decades, they have mesmerized children and entertained adults. Dinosaurs are pictured on television, in books, in classrooms, in movies, in magazines, and on all sorts of paraphernalia. Advertisers use them to sell everything from oatmeal to hamburgers and board games to piggy banks.

Those mysterious reptiles known as dinosaurs have captivated not just our nation, but the entire world. In 1956, Godzilla made the big screen come alive with his city-crushing tirades. Since that time, dinosaurs have made an appearance on untold millions of soda cans, cereal boxes, posters, and other such items. For years, absorbent little minds have flocked to television to watch their favorite purple dinosaur, Barney, bounce around the stage, teaching them to pick up their toys, and say "please" and "thank you."

At the writing of this book, dinosaur-saturated material continues to flood the market—a trend that likely will carry on for years to come. Take, for instance, the Wendy's™ children's meal bag that has a 2001 copyright date. From this beautifully colored, slick-papered bag, hungry young readers can learn about dinosaurs like *Stegosaurus*, *Oviraptor*, and the infamous *Tyrannosaurus rex*. Or what about the Large Aqua Dinosaur Big Belly™ Bank? This exciting collector's bank features a free-standing dinosaur with a large, clear belly that holds coins. In order for the coins to get into the belly, children "feed" the coins through the mouth of the money-hungry dinosaur, and then watch the coins roll down the meandering throat canal into the belly below. And if that does not satisfy your child's dinosaur cravings, you can order an inflatable, enclosed trampoline shaped like a dinosaur. Also available is the ever-popular board game, "The Dinosaur Game," that boasts of having won 11 awards, and was featured on "Good Morning America." Other dinosaur products on the market include countless books, one of which is named *Dinosaurs Divorce*. It purports to help divorcing parents teach their children about their situation by using a family of dinosaurs. This animal is

On a Wendy's™ kids' meal bag, an unsuspecting child can learn of the alleged "fact" that "birds are probably related to dinosaurs."

so popular with children that it often has its own section at the bookstore. What other animal do you know that frequently has its own section in the bookstore?

And we must not forget the ever-growing number of movies starring these captivating creatures. The landmark movie, *Jurassic Park*, drew children and adults to the box office by the millions, and its two successors, *The Lost World* and *Jurassic Park 3*, raked in tens-of-millions of dollars. Not least on the list of critically acclaimed dinosaur movies was the Walt Disney classic titled, appropriately, *Dinosaur*. One reviewer of *Dinosaur* stated that "kids will love the film," and noted that the film, which was "geared primarily towards a younger audience," was "aimed squarely at the under-10 crowd."

People are fascinated with dinosaurs, and the various companies and agencies that want to turn a quick dollar are smart enough to seize upon that fascination. Unfortunately, however, dinosaurs are not used just to make money. These marvelous creatures also have been laden with a backbreaking load of evolutionary baggage. For decades, dinosaurs have been exploited by evolutionists and used to spread false evolutionary propaganda. As evidence of this fact, consider that on that same aforementioned Wendy's™ kids' meal bag, an unsuspecting child can learn the alleged "fact" that "birds are probably related to dinosaurs." A person can see, via the timeline on the side panel of the bag, that dinosaurs first appeared "245 million years ago," and then became extinct

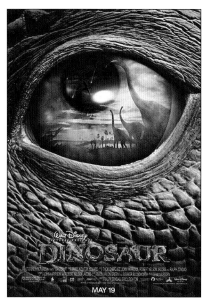

"64 million years ago." And the same movie reviewer who mentioned that *Dinosaur* was aimed at the "under-10 crowd," also noted that the movie was set "65 million years ago during the late Cretaceous period."

What is wrong with this information? Notice that no humans are depicted in the *Dinosaur* animation. Such is the case because, according to evolutionary theory, humans did not evolve until about three million years ago, separating them from the dinosaurs by an alleged 62 million years or so. This concept, however, stands in direct contradiction to biblical teaching, which states that God made dinosaurs on day six of the Creation (since dinosaurs, by definition, are land-living animals)—the exact same day that He made humans. Furthermore, Jesus Himself stated that Adam and Eve, the first humans, had been on Earth "from the beginning of creation" (Mark 10:6), not millions of years removed from it.

Currently, the sad state of affairs finds the amazing creatures we know as dinosaurs being hijacked by those who use them to teach evolution-based concepts. In contradistinction, when God was in the midst of His discussion with Job (Job 40-41), He mentioned two creatures—behemoth and leviathan—that resemble either dinosaurs or dinosaur-like animals. God, however, referred to these creatures to impress upon Job His unfathomable power—the exact opposite of what dinosaurs are being used to teach today.

We are frequently compelled, year after year, to write and lecture about these extinct reptiles, not because of their popularity, but because of the major role they play in teaching evolutionary theory. More than anything else, **dinosaurs are the poster children of evolution.** What the gecko is to Geico® or the duck to Aflac®, dinosaurs are to evolution. Consider a couple of examples of their evolutionary "poster child" status. On the cover of the popular toddler's pop-up book titled *Life on Earth*, a baby is holding a rattle, crawling along the nose

of a dinosaur. The book begins with these words: "The very first living things came from the sea." Later children learn that "[s]ome fish crawled out of the water and became amphibians." After viewing a few pictures of dinosaurs, which supposedly evolved from amphibians, kids "discover" that "[t]hen people appeared," although "[t]hey were a bit hairy at first." Finally, the back cover of the book shows a baby sliding down the tail of a dinosaur with the following emphatic words above him: "Millions of years ago life on Earth started in the oceans. Then it moved onto the land and eventually led to YOU!" (Holmes, 2002). This is the picture so often painted with dinosaurs. They are used to teach evolution in a fun, "you-don't-want-to-miss-it" kind of way. Sadly, FamilyFun.com described this book as a "fantastic and super-fun reading experience" (see Butler and Kratz, n.d.), and listed it among the "22 Best Children's Books of 2002." Apparently, using dinosaurs to teach children that their

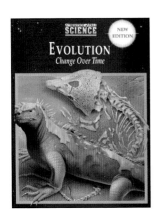

great-great-great-great...grandparents crawled out of water and onto land millions of years ago makes a "fascinating" reading experience.

In the widely used, 100-page middle school science textbook titled *Evolution–Change Over Time* (published by Prentice Hall), attempts are made to establish evolution as a fact by using a variety of alleged proofs. One piece of "evidence," however, that appears on nearly **one out of every three pages** centers on dinosaurs. The first two chapters in this three-chapter textbook begin with pictures and text about dinosaurs. In several sections of the book (in which the main thrust is not about dinosaurs), students are asked to participate in reading or writing activities that focus on dinosaurs. Truly, the authors and editors of this "science" textbook (which once was used throughout the United States) have attempted to indoctrinate young minds with the "truths" of evolution by using dinosaurs more than anything else.

Dinosaurs are so entwined with evolutionary thinking that in his anti-creationist book titled, *Abusing Science: The Case Against Creationism*, evolutionist Philip Kitcher admitted that solid evidence for the co-existence of dinosaurs and humans would **"shake the foundations of evolutionary theory**, because, of course, the dinosaurs are supposed to have been long extinct by the time the hominids arrived on the scene" (1982, p. 121, emp. added). Why would proof of dinosaur and human cohabitation "shake the foundations of evolutionary theory" if dinosaurs were not so fundamental to the theory's promotion? Obviously, they are.

Inarguably, dinosaurs are the "sugar stick" that evolutionists use to capture the attention of both young and old alike. This book represents our effort to provide a well-researched, logical, biblical, and scientifically accurate case that counteracts and refutes the "evolutionary dinosaur argument." Obviously, if nearly one-third of the pages in a student's evolutionary science textbook contains information about dinosaurs, young people are going to have questions about these creatures in light of what the Bible teaches. And, considering how many feature articles in *National Geographic, Discover, Science*, etc., have to do with dinosaurs, many adults have similar questions. Once

during a seminar near a large University outside of Chicago, a longtime professor, who was a Christian, came to the lecture series with one question. "I just have one question," he said. "What about the dinosaurs? Can you tell me about the dinosaurs?" This gentleman had been a professor for more than 25 years. He was a very educated man with a distinguished career. But, dinosaurs were an enigma.

Indeed, adults do wonder about dinosaurs. They have questions left over from their childhood years. They have questions about the latest *National Geographic* article that talks about dinosaurs living millions of years before humans. And they have a catalog of questions that their children have asked, which they may never have gotten around to answering. Did these reptiles evolve millions of years ago, or did God create them? Are humans separated from the time of the dinosaurs by 60+ million years, or did God create both humans and dinosaurs on day six of Creation? How could humans have lived with such terrifying creatures? Is there any evidence that humans and dinosaurs once lived together? What happened to the dinosaurs? Doesn't the fossil record prove dinosaurs and humans never lived together? Etc.

We believe that evolutionists have had their way with dinosaurs long enough. It is essential for creationists to dispel the "evolutionary aura" surrounding these creatures, and see them for what they really are–testimonies of an Almighty God Who made them alongside His image-bearers (humans–Genesis 1:26-27) during the Creation week (just like the Bible says!).

CHAPTER 2

Historical Evidence for the Coexistence of Dinosaurs and Humans—Part 1

If dinosaurs and humans once walked the Earth together (as the Bible implies–Exodus 20:11), it is logical to conclude that humans would have left behind at least two different types of evidence. First, similar to how we take pictures of places we visit and wildlife we see in modern times, people living hundreds or thousands of years ago (before the invention of cameras) would likely have drawn or carved pictures of dinosaurs, as well as many other animals (see chapters 4 and 5 for examples of such ancient drawings). Second, just as we tell stories today of interesting things that we have seen and heard, the ancients would have told stories about dinosaurs, if they ever encountered these creatures. Do such stories exist? Is there historical support for the coexistence of dinosaurs and humans? You be the judge.

LEGENDS

Oftentimes people refer to stories of the distant past as "legends." *The American Heritage Dictionary of the English Language* defines "legend" as "1a. An unverified story handed down from earlier times, especially one popularly believed to be historical. b. A body or collection of such stories. c. A romanticized or popularized myth of modern times" (2000, p. 1000). Although sometimes told in a believable fashion, many legends, no doubt, are pure fantasy. They are filled with imaginary people and animals performing all sorts of unbelievable, magical, mythical deeds. Santa Claus flying through the air with his reindeer on the eve of December 25 delivering gifts all over the world; Rip Van Winkle sleeping for 20 years under a shade tree; or Paul Bunyan and his blue ox creating Minnesota's lakes with their giant footprints–all could be categorized as legendary characters performing imaginary feats. Legends of mermaids, sphinxes, and centaurs also can be safely classified as pure fantasy.

Other legends, however, are not so fanciful. Stories that are ubiquitous, included in reputable, historical writings as factual, and supported by science cannot reasonably be disregarded as "just unbelievable legends." Take, for example, the legend of a worldwide flood. Stories have surfaced in hundreds of cultures

throughout the world that tell of a huge, catastrophic flood which destroyed most of mankind, and that was survived only by a few individuals and animals (Perloff, 1999, p. 167). The Babylonians, Greeks, Chinese, Aztecs, Toltecs, and many others have variations of the flood story. According to evolutionary geologist Robert Schoch, "Noah is but one tale in a worldwide collection of at least 500 flood myths" (2003, p. 249). Canadian geologist, Sir William Dawson, wrote about how the record of the Flood "is preserved in some of the oldest historical documents of several distinct races of men, and is indirectly corroborated by the whole tenor of the early history of most of the civilized races" (1895, pp. 4ff.). Even

the most well-preserved book of antiquity, the Bible, which Christians believe to be the truthful, inspired Word of God, testifies repeatedly that a worldwide flood engulfed the Earth in the days of the patriarch Noah (Genesis 6-8; Isaiah 54:9; Matthew 24:36-39; Luke 17:26-27; 1 Peter 3:20). What's more, much scientific evidence exists suggesting the occurrence of a universal flood sometime in the past. In their book *The Genesis Flood*, John Whitcomb and Henry Morris spent nearly 100 pages presenting such data (1961, pp. 116-211). Worldwide stories of a worldwide flood? Preserved in some of the oldest historical documents, including the Bible? Corroborated by an assortment of scientific facts? Though various details in the hundreds of worldwide flood legends have been tainted over time with multiple errors and contradictions (e.g., the Aztecs' legend that indicates only two people survived the global Flood rather than eight), there are logical reasons to believe that the general outlines of flood legends are true and testify to the Bible's reliability.

DRAGON LEGENDS

But what about dinosaurs? Is there any evidence from history that humans lived with these giant reptiles from the past? Are there stories of humans interacting with large reptilian creatures that possessed massive tails, fearsome teeth, hefty legs, horned heads, and spiked backs?

Indeed, a wide variety of stories of large reptiles have been passed down through the ages from cultures all over the world. Many of these creatures sound very much like dinosaurs, or dinosaur-like (marine or flying) reptiles (e.g., *plesiosaurus* and *pterodactyl*). However, these animals are never called dinosaurs in the stories. Since the term "dinosaur" (from the Greek words *deinos*, meaning "fearfully great," and *sauros*, meaning "lizard" or "reptile") was not coined until the early 1840s (when fossilized dinosaur bones were first discovered and reconstructed in modern times), stories told previously of "fearfully great reptiles" could not have included the word "dinosaur." Instead, the name attached to these creatures was

"dragon." Have some dragon legends been embellished over time? Of course. Just as people today tend to embellish the size of fish they catch or the size of a dog that nips their leg, people in the past said things about dragons that undoubtedly were exaggerations. Such inaccuracies, however, do not negate the overriding truth that "fearfully great reptiles" of many different shapes and sizes once lived with humans–any more than the differences in worldwide flood legends mean we must discount the idea of a universal flood.

THE UBIQUITY AND ANTIQUITY OF DRAGON LEGENDS

Were legends of large dinosaur-like reptiles only to appear in a handful of cultures around the world late in history, one might well argue for their dismissal in legitimate historical discussions. After all, what is a smattering of strange animal descriptions and fairy-tale-like stories interspersed in only a few places on Earth? Such similar stories of unique reptilian creatures in only a handful of places on the globe might reasonably be passed off as just coincidence. The "coincidence card," however, looks rather weak in light of the vast amount of testimony regarding the longstanding, widespread nature of dragon legends.

Many authors are adamant that dragons were purely mythical creatures. Yet, interestingly, these same writers testify to the ubiquity of dragon legends. Take, for example, Carl Lindall, contributing writer for *World Book Encyclopedia*. He believes "[d]ragons did not really exist," even though "[e]**very country** had them in its mythology. In Greece dragons were slain by Hercules, Apollo, and Perseus. Sigurd, Siegfried, and Beowulf killed them in Norse, German, and English legend" (1996, 5:265-266, emp. added). In his brief book on *Chinese Dragons*, Roy Bates, like Lindall, suggested that the dragon "was never a real beast" (2002, p. 15). Yet, Bates similarly confessed: "**No other creature in the world** has had such a far-reaching influence on the minds of so many people" (p. vii, emp. added). A 1981 *Science Digest* article, titled "The Spread of Dragon Myths," informed readers, "as myth they [dragons–EL/KB] are among the most…persistent and widespread in the world. From millennium to millennium and over all the earth's continents, dragon and serpent lore shows remarkable similarity" (1981, 89:103). Still, *Science Digest* was adamant that "[d]ragons, of course, are myth" (89:103).

Several others also have testified to the widespread nature of dragon legends. The famed 20th-century evolutionist, Carl Sagan, noted: "The implacable mutual hostility between man and dragon, as exemplified in the myth of St. George is strongest in the West…. But it is not a Western anomaly. **It is a worldwide phenomenon**" (1977, p. 150, emp. added). Militant evolutionist and *LiveScience.com* staff writer Ker Than admitted: "Dragons are…found in the myths and legends of cultures all around the world" (2007). James Perloff wrote:

> The Flood is not the only common remembrance of the world's cultures. They also remember 'dragons.' From England to China, these were a long part of national 'mythologies.' The Indians of North and South America had legends about them. They were written of in Ireland, France, Germany, Italy, Greece, Switzerland, Scandinavia, Ethiopia, Egypt, Persia, Russia, India, and Japan (1999, p. 181).

On the inside front dust jacket of his book, *Dragon: A Natural History*, Dr. Karl Shuker noted that dragons "have been found in an astounding number of places. Dragons and their near relatives have found niches in every ecosystem on the planet–from the mountains of Greece to the forests of northern Europe to the volcanic plain of Mesoamerica to the river valleys of China–and have, as a consequence, become deeply embedded in human culture" (1995). Shuker even included a world map showing the existence of dragon legends in cultures on every continent except Antarctica (pp. 6-7). Daniel Cohen called the dragon "the most common monster in the world…. People all over the world have believed in dragons" (1975, p. 97). "A thousand years ago dragons were such familiar creatures that what they looked like and how they behaved was common knowledge to every man, woman, and child," wrote Dr. Peter Hogarth and Val Cleary in their book *Dragons* (1979, p. 12). They contin-

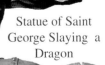

Statue of Saint George Slaying a Dragon

ued: "No matter where they lived, everyone could describe dragons and dragon behavior..." (p. 12). In her book, *British Dragons,* Jacqueline Simpson mentioned how in Great Britain alone some 80 dragon legends have been uncovered (1980, p. 10). "Over 70 villages and small towns [in Great Britain–EL/KB] still have a tradition about a local dragon, or can be shown on good evidence to have had such a tradition in the past" (p. 9).

Compsognathus

In 2005, *Animal Planet* aired a program (which they later released on DVD) titled *Dragons: A Fantasy Made Real.* The film incorporated legend, alleged scientific facts, various theories (including, and especially, evolution), state-of-the-art CGI animation, and the voice talent of Patrick Stewart. It was a highly publicized film that once again put a spotlight on dragons. Although it was far from a legitimate documentary, several statements from the film reinforce the ubiquitous nature of dragon stories. Within the first minute of the program, the viewer learns:

> There is one creature remembered in the legends of almost every human culture that's ever existed. A creature depicted with remarkable similarity by the Chinese, the Aztecs, even the Inuit who live in a frozen land where no reptiles are found–even they have stories of this animal: the dragon. Cultures from different continents, people who had no contact with one another yet all of them have stories describing the same mythical animal (*Dragons: A Fantasy…*, 2005a).

The dragon is "a creature that burns bright in the memory of all humankind" (2005a). "People that could have never spoken to one another shared visions of the same creature"–the dragon (*Dragons: A Fantasy…*, 2005b). On the back cover of the *Dragons* DVD, *Animal Planet* highlighted how "[t]hroughout human history, people have been fascinated with dragons, which have appeared in the myths and legends of almost every world culture" (2005a). Although, admittedly, *Dragons: A Fantasy Made Real* was more "docu-fantasy" than documentary, the repeated comments about the world's immersion into dragon lore are backed by an enormous reserve of testimony. All historians and dragon lovers seem to be in agreement on at least this one point: **reports of dragon legends are universal**.

Dragon legends also are characterized by their longstanding tradition. According to *The New Encyclopedia Britannica*, "**From ancient times**, it [the Chinese dragon–EL/KB] was the emblem of the Imperial family, and until the founding of the republic (1911) the dragon adorned the Chinese flag" ("Dragon," 1997, 4:209, emp. added; see also Bates, 2002, p. vii). In his book, *History Begins at Sumer*, Dr. Samuel Kramer observed how "the dragon-slaying theme was an important motif in the Sumerian my-thology **of the third mil-lennium B.C.**" (1959, p. 170, emp. added). "**[F]our**

Tanystropheus longobardicus

21

thousand years ago," Hogarth and Clery wrote, "sightings of dragons seem to have been almost as frequent as sightings of whales today" (1979, p. 13). Dragons are anything but new. Unlike new breeds of dogs and other animals which seem to pop up every few years, the dragon seems always to have been in the mind of man. *Animal Planet* admitted: "This is the animal about which humankind has **throughout our history** been most compelled by" (*Dragons: A Fantasy…*, 2005a, emp. added). Though we would highly disagree with *Science Digest's* extended, evolutionary timetable, notice what the journal suggested about the antiquity of dragon legends: "[T]he earliest dragonlike [sic] myths may have originated as long as **100,000 years ago.…** As myth they [dragons–EL/KB] are among **the most ancient.…** Dragon legends have been with humanity **since the dawn of recorded history…**" ("The Spread…," 1981, 89:103, emp. added). Dragon legends are not just cute stories that our ancestors began telling only in the last few centuries. They have been told all over the world for millennia. Such antiquity and ubiquity deserves an adequate explanation.

THE VARIETY OF DRAGONS

The English word dragon is derived from the Greek word *drakon* via the Latin *draco*, which "was used originally for any large serpent" ("Dragon," 1997, 4:209) or reptile (Hogarth and Clery, 1979, p. 80), whether real or mythological, aquatic, aerial, or terrestrial. [NOTE: The Greek legend of Medea flying through the air in a chariot pulled by dragons indicates

that even in Greek culture something more than just large snakes was often implied by the use of *drakon*.] In English, "dragon" came to mean a creature that was "basically reptilian," though with a variety of possible features, such as wings, legs, claws, horns, etc. (cf. Simpson, 1980, p. 14). The forms of dragons "varied from the earliest of times," but its reptilian traits were always dominant ("Dragon," 1997, 4:209).

In his book, *Dragons: A Natural History*, Dr. Shuker observed: "For although the winged, four-legged, flame-spewing horror of classical mythology may well be the most

Image of Sirrush as depicted on the Ishtar Gate

famous type of dragon in the Western world, it is far from being the only type on record" (1995, p. 9). Daniel Cohen agreed, saying, "[T]here are many kinds of dragons" (1975, p. 97). Tiamat of ancient Babylon was said to have a scaly body, four legs, and wings ("Dragon," 1997, 4:209). Sirrush was depicted in Babylon with four legs, scales, a horned head, and a snake-like tongue. Chinese dragons have "a long, scaly, serpentine neck and body," as well as four legs, but they are mostly wingless (Rose, 2000, p. 279). According to Hogarth and Clery, Chinese dragons were said to have resembled each other in nine ways, more or less: "The horns resemble those of a stag, his head that of a camel, his eyes those of a demon, his neck that of a snake, his belly that of a clam, his scales those of a carp, his claw those of an eagle, his soles like those of a tiger, his ears those of a cow" (1979, p. 53). Western dragons, like the oriental dragons, had large, scale-covered, elongated bodies with two or four legs, and tails. Unlike most of the Eastern dragons, however, many of the Western dragons had "vast wings like those of a bat" (Rose, 2000, p. 104), and some had crested heads.

Wales, whose national flag predominately displays a red dragon (an animal associated with the country for centuries), reportedly once had many reptiles occupying its airspace. According to Marie Trevelyan:

National Flag of Wales

> The woods round Penllyne Castle, Glamorgan, had the reputation of being frequent-ed by winged serpents, and these were the terror of old and young alike…. Some of them had crests sparkling with all the colours of the rainbow. When disturbed they glided swiftly…to their hiding places. When angry, they flew over peoples' heads, with outspread wings bright…like the features in a peacock's tail (as quoted in Simpson, 1980, p. 34).

After being wounded, one of these "winged serpents" was said to have begun "beating its assailant about the head with its wings" (p. 34).

In the English epic *Beowulf,* more than 1,000 years old, the hero is said to have encountered a "fearsome earth-dragon." It was described as a "crooked, coiled worm" that "flies through the night, enveloped in flame," causing men to "fear him greatly." As the story goes, Beowulf killed the beast, but not before its

Dimorphodon

venomous bite ultimately led to his own doom (see Simpson, 1980, pp. 28-29).

Two well-known ancient historians have documented that flying reptiles and humans were contemporaries more than 2,000 years ago. Herodotus, a respected Greek historian who lived in approximately 450 B.C., once wrote:

> There is a place in Arabia...to which I went, on hearing of some **winged serpents**; and when I arrived there, I saw bones and spines of serpents, in such quantities as it would be impossible to describe. The form of the serpent is like that of a water-snake; but **he has wings without feathers**, and **as like as possible to the wings of a bat** (n.d., emp. added).

Herodotus recognized that such creatures were not birds, mammals, or insects—but reptiles with wings. In the first

century A.D. the Jewish historian Josephus wrote about Moses and the Israelites having a difficult time passing through a particular region because of the presence of flying reptiles:

> When the ground was difficult to be passed over, because of the multitude of serpents (which it produces in vast numbers...**some** of which ascend out of the ground unseen, and also **fly in the air**,

Herodotus

25

Josephus

air, and do come upon men at unawares, and do them a mischief)....

[Moses] made baskets like unto arks, of sedge, and filled them with ibes [i.e., birds], and carried them along with them; which animal is the greatest enemy to **serpents** imaginable, for **they fly from them when they come near them**; and **as they fly** they are caught and devoured by them (1987, 2:10:2, emp. added).

Although these two historians did not mention the extremely large flying reptiles, they did record snake-like, winged creatures that could fly.

In the 1200s, Italian explorer Marco Polo wrote of seeing long, two-legged reptiles (called "lindworms") while passing through Central Asia (n.d., 2:49). Time-Life reported how one ancient Chinese emperor of the Sung Dynasty (c. A.D. 1000-1300) is said to have raised a dragon in his palace (*Dragons...*, 1984, p. 57). According to a chronicle in Canterbury Cathedral, around A.D. 1449, Englishmen reported seeing "two fire-breathing dragons engaged in a fierce, hour-long struggle." One was black, while the other was "reddish and spotted" (*Folklore...*, 1973, p. 241). In her book *British Dragons*, Jacqueline Simpson brings to light several dragon legends, including one that in 1866 was reported to have originally occurred in 1405.

Painting of a *Pteranodon*

Pteranodon had a wingspan of over 23 feet.

Close to the town of Bures, near Sudbury, there has lately appeared, to the great hurt of the countryside, **a dragon, vast in body, with a crested head, teeth like a saw, and a tail, extending to an enormous length.** Having slaughtered the shepherd of a flock, it devoured many sheep. There came forth in order to shoot at him with arrows the workmen of the lord on whose estate he had concealed himself, being Sir Richard de Waldegrave, Knight; but the dragon's body, although struck by the archers, remained unhurt, for **the arrows bounced off his back as if it were iron or hard rock.** Those arrows that fell upon the spine of his back gave out as they struck it a ringing of tinkling sound, just as if they had hit a brazen plate, and then flew away off by reason of the hide of this great beast being impenetrable. Thereupon, in order to destroy him, all the country people around were summoned. But when the dragon saw that he was again about to be assailed with arrows, he fled into a marsh or mere and there hid himself among the long reeds, and was no more seen (p. 60, emp. added).

Although some will continue to dismiss all dragons as purely mythical creatures, the widely purported eyewitness accounts of these animals indicate otherwise. In his foreword to Dr. Shuker's book, *Dragons: A Natural History*, Desmond Morris remarked: "As recently as the seventeenth century, scholars wrote of dragons as though they were scientific fact, their anatomy and natural history being recorded in painstaking detail" (Shuker, 1995, p. 8). Hogarth and Clery agreed, saying, "No matter where they lived, everyone could describe dragons and dragon behavior in colorfully lurid detail" (1979, p. 12). They continued:

> The evidence [for dragons—EL/KB] is not confined to works of natural history and literature but appears in everyday chronicles of events…. And such eyewitness accounts are not derived from hearsay or anonymous rumor; they were set down by people of some standing, by kings and knights, monks and archbishops, scholars and saints (1979, pp. 13-14).

Even *Animal Planet* could not help but be impressed by the voluminous amount of documentation for these animals. In their 2005 film on dragons they expressed amazement over "how much was known about dragons…. All the different kinds of dragons. **And it's all documented in medieval manuscripts and Chinese encyclopedias**" (2005a, emp. added). One of the producers of the film even asked: "Everyday of the week Animal Planet tells you about all the animals around this planet that we live on. **But what about the one animal that we all know about, the one animal that we all grew up with, the one animal that's in popular culture around the world?**" (2005a, emp. added). Why do more people not consider these animals as historical? After all, as consultant Dr. Peter Hogarth pointed out, "People believed in dragons as real animals, just like any other animal. And,

actually if you think about it, how could you say in Western Europe in the Middle Ages that an elephant was a real animal and a dragon wasn't? The information you had about them was both the same in each case" (2005a).

Even the Bible–the most historically documented, widely read ancient book in all the world–describes dragon-like animals. Like Herodotus and Josephus, it mentions the "flying serpent" (Isaiah 30:6). In Job 40, God described a behemoth with bones "like bars of bronze,…ribs like bars of iron" (vs. 18) whose tail "moves…like a cedar" (vs. 17). This behemoth was "chief of the ways of God" (vs. 19, ASV). Though there likely was much speculation about this animal, since he apparently lived a more secluded life "under the lotus trees, in a covert of reeds and marsh" (vs. 21), it was no fairytale creature, for God told Job that, the behemoth, "I made along with you" (vs. 15).

Still, perhaps more notable than the massive behemoth is the creature that God described next. In speaking to Job about His sovereignty over the natural world, Jehovah described a real animal called leviathan. God began by asking several rhetorical questions:

> Can you draw out leviathan with a hook, or snare his tongue with a line which you lower? Can you put a reed through his nose, or pierce his jaw with a hook? Will he make many supplications to you? Will he speak softly to you? Will he make a covenant with you? Will you take him as a servant forever? Will you play with him as with a bird, or will you leash him for your maidens? Will your companions make

"Leviathan" by Lewis Lavoie

a banquet of him? Will they apportion him among the merchants? Can you fill his skin with harpoons, or his head with fishing spears? Lay your hand on him; remember the battle–never do it again! Indeed, any hope of overcoming him is false; shall one not be overwhelmed at the sight of him? No one is so fierce that he would dare stir him up…. I will not conceal his limbs, his mighty power, or his graceful proportions. Who can remove his outer coat? Who can approach him with a double bridle? Who can

open the doors of his face, with his terrible teeth all around (41:1-14)?

Job could do none of these things. Through poetic language, God obviously was reminding Job of leviathan's renowned strength and ferocity. God continued his description of leviathan, saying,

His rows of scales are his pride, shut up tightly as with a seal; one is so near another that no air can come between them; they are joined one to another, they stick together and cannot be parted. His sneezings flash forth light, and his eyes are like the eyelids of the morning. Out of his mouth go burning lights; sparks of fire shoot out. Smoke goes out of his nostrils, as from a boiling pot and burning rushes. His breath kindles coals, and a flame goes out of his mouth. Strength dwells in his neck, and sorrow dances before him. The folds of his flesh are joined together; they are firm on him and cannot be moved. His heart is as hard as stone, even as hard as the lower millstone. When he raises himself up, the mighty are afraid; because of his crashings they are beside themselves. Though the sword reaches him, it cannot avail; nor does spear, dart, or javelin. He regards iron as straw, and bronze as rotten wood. The arrow cannot make him flee; slingstones become like stubble to him. Darts are regarded as straw; he laughs at the threat of javelins. His undersides are like sharp potsherds; He spreads pointed marks in the mire. He makes the deep boil like a pot; he makes the sea like a pot of ointment. He leaves a shining wake behind him; one would think the deep had white hair. On earth there is nothing like him, which is made without fear. He beholds every high thing; He is king over all the children of pride (41:15-34).

Could a better description of a dragon be found anywhere? Leviathan had mighty power, an extremely strong neck, "terrible teeth all around," tightly joined rows of scales that were virtually impenetrable, and a jagged underside that left pointed marks on the ground when it came up on land. Most impressive was its ability to expel "sparks of fire" from its mouth and "smoke" from its nose. Were this found in a book of mythology, one might chalk it up to fantasy. However, leviathan and behemoth were anything but mythical (see chapter 6). These creatures are recorded in the Bible, not a book of fables and mythology, and they were described by God Himself. What's more, these creatures were described in a context where many other real animals were mentioned, including the horse, the hawk, and the ostrich (Job 38-39). Finally, if behemoth and leviathan were, in fact, make-believe, God's entire speech (regarding His sovereignty over the created world) would be pointless.

CHAPTER 3

Historical Evidence for the Coexistence of Dinosaurs and Humans—Part 2

So what were dragons? The stories about them are worldwide. They are recorded in reputable, historical writings as factual. If one cannot reasonably dismiss all of these creatures with a mere wave of the hand, what could they have been? Are there any animals alive today that resemble dragons? Or, are there any good candidates that are now extinct?

In an article titled "Top 10 Beasts and Dragons: How Reality Made Myth," evolutionist Ker Than explored "what may have inspired the look of dragons" (2007). He first proposed that "Chinese alligators may have been one of the inspirations for the Asian dragon" (2007). Other nominees included the three-foot frill-neck lizard, the 20-inch bearded dragon, the seven-inch flying dragon (which uses wing-like folds of skin to jump from tree to tree), the 18-inch fish we call a sea dragon, the 10-foot-long Komodo dragon, and the 30-foot python. Incredibly, Than's number one explanation for dragon legends centered around– not animals–but comets.

> To people living in ancient times, a comet streaking through the skies with an icy tail millions of miles long would have closely resembled such a creature…. If comets were the inspiration for some dragons, it could help explain why dragons are ubiquitous in the myths and legends of so many different cultures in all corners of the world (2007).

A comet? The litany of dragon legends around the world is indebted to comets for their existence? Such an explanation borders on the ridiculous. Suggesting that small lizards were the inspiration for one of man's most dreaded, worldwide foes seems equally absurd. Pythons and certain alligators certainly can be frightening, and undoubtedly were considered formidable foes, but they simply do not fit the characteristics of many of the dragons described throughout history. Though komodo dragons are intimidating creatures, even Than admitted the unlikelihood of them being the inspiration of European dragons since "Europeans didn't discover them until 1910" (2007).

Surprisingly, Than acknowledged:

> **Of all the creatures that ever lived, pterosaurs probably most closely resemble the dragons of European legend.** Reptilian and featherless, pterosaurs flew on wings of hide that were supported by a single long and boney finger. The smallest pterosaur was the size of a sparrow, while Quetzalcoatlus–named after the Aztec god–had a wingspan of more than 40 feet, making it the largest flying creature ever (2007, emp. added).

Indeed, extinct dinosaur-like flying reptiles (e.g., *Quetzalcoatlus, Rhamphorhynchus,* and *Pterodactyl*) with two legs, large wingspans,

Quetzalcoatlus

Which one looks more like a dragon to you?

claws, slender tails, and toothed beaks more closely resemble many dragons, by a considerable margin, than any animal alive today. One wonders how Than could make such a statement and still list pterosaurs as number three on his top-10 list of what gave rise to dragon legends.

Could dinosaurs or dinosaur-like marine or flying reptiles really be the inspiration for dragon legends? Although Carl

Dracorex

Lindall believes that the animals which inspired dragon legends "did not really exist," he confessed that "dragons of legend are **strangely** like actual creatures that have lived in the past.... They are **much like** the great reptiles which inhabited the earth long before man is supposed to have appeared on Earth" (1996, 5:265, emp. added). *The New Encyclopedia Britannica* referred to dinosaurs as "gigantic, prehistoric, **dragon-like** reptiles," yet the encyclopedia was careful to say that dragon legends "apparently arose without the slightest knowledge on the part of the ancients" of these real animals ("Dragon," 1997, 4:209, emp. added).

Dragons and dinosaurs also gave Daniel Cohen difficulty. He admitted what so many people know all too well:

> **No creature that ever lived looked more like dragons than dinosaurs.** Like the dragons, dinosaurs were huge reptiles. Dinosaurs themselves didn't fly, but at the time of the dinosaurs, there were a number of large flying reptiles.... It sounds as though the dragon legend could have begun with the dinosaurs. Through the ages, stories about dinosaurs would have been confused and exaggerated (1975, pp. 104,106, emp. added).

In 2003, a nearly complete dinosaur skull was excavated in the Hell Creek Formation in South Dakota. The long, knobby, spiky skull appeared so similar to descriptions and

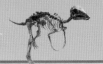

paintings of certain "legendary" dragons, it actually was named *Dracorex*, meaning "dragon king" (see Bakker, et al., 2006). The Children's Museum of Indianapolis, which now possesses the skull, referred to it as "a new type of dinosaur" that is "66-million-years-old" and "**looks like a dragon**" ("Dracorex...," n.d., emp. added). The Children's Museum displayed a placard next to a *Dracorex* image that read: "When we saw this creature's head, we weren't sure what kind of dinosaur it was. Its spiky horns, bumps and long muzzle **looked more like a dragon**" ("Dracorex...," n.d., emp. added). A dinosaur that looks more like a dragon? Interesting.

Dr. Shuker also recognized that "[s]ome dragons were clearly inspired by real-life animals long familiar to the zoological world" (1995, p. 10). He later connected dragons with dinosaurs, saying, "**There is no doubt** that dragons and certain dinosaurs (especially some of the larger predatory types) do exhibit a **surprising** outward similarity" (p. 93 emp. added). The truth is, the only reason to reject what appears so obvious and be "surprised" by the similarities between dragons and dinosaurs, is if a person buys

Used with permission from the Children's Museum of Indianapolis

into the evolutionary timeline. Cohen confessed: "The problem is time. As far as we know, all the dinosaurs died out over 70 million years ago. That long ago, there were no people on the earth. So who could remember the dinosaurs?" (1975, p. 106).

Renowned atheist Carl Sagan speculated that humans may very well "remember" dinosaurs. He recognized the ubiquity of dragon legends and indicated that the "pervasiveness" of these stories "is probably no accident" (1977, p. 149). Interestingly, Sagan hypothesized that "dragons posed a problem for our protohuman ancestors of a few million years ago, and that the terror they evoked and the deaths they caused helped bring about the evolution of human intelligence" (p. 150). Sagan then specifically addressed dinosaurs and dragons. He wrote:

> The most recent dinosaur fossil is dated at about sixty million years ago. The family of man (but not the genus *Homo*) is some tens of millions of years old. Could there have been manlike creatures who actually encountered *Tyrannosaurus rex*? Could there have been dinosaurs that escaped the extinctions in the late Cretaceous Period? Could the pervasive dreams and common fear of "monsters," which children develop shortly after they are able to talk, be evolutionary vestiges of quite adaptive–baboonlike–responses to dragons and owls? (Sagan, 1977, p. 151).

The spikes and horns of *Euoplacephalus* were very "dragonesque."

Notice that even Carl Sagan, one of the foremost evolutionists of the 20th century, could not get around the fact that dragons sound eerily similar to dinosaurs. Such speculations on the origin of dragons would be meaningless unless one believed that dragons and dinosaurs appear to be one and the same. Still, the best explanation that Sagan could conjure up, while still holding onto some semblance of the evolutionary geologic timetable, is that our very early "baboonlike" ancestors encountered dinosaurs (who may have "escaped the extinctions in the late Cretaceous Period") and passed their memories of them on down to modern man. Once again, we find evolutionists' explanations of dragon legends bizarre, irrational, and even laughable. If it were not for evolutionists' commitment to their faulty billion-year timetable (see "The Geologic…," 2003; see also DeYoung, 2005), it would appear they would have few problems accepting what is so obvious–that dinosaurs previously were called dragons, and humans once lived with them on Earth.

FIRE-BREATHING DRAGONS?

So, if dragons were dinosaurs, does that mean that dinosaurs breathed fire? After all, some dragon legends speak of these creatures expelling smoke and/or fire from their mouths. Even the Bible describes leviathan as a fire-breathing animal. Is this as absurd as suggesting that our alleged animal ancestors passed down their memories of dinosaurs over tens of millions of years or that dragon legends originated from comets in outer space? Not at all. Read on.

In his 1998 book titled, *The Genesis Question*, well-known progressive creationist Hugh Ross insisted that "[n]o dinosaur... ever breathed fire or smoke," and he ridiculed the idea that leviathan was a dinosaur or dinosaur-like aquatic creature that breathed fire (p. 48). (Ross chose rather to believe that the magnificent creature described by God in His second speech

to Job was a crocodile; see chapter 6 for a response to such a suggestion.) How can Ross or anyone else be so certain that "no dinosaur...ever breathed fire or smoke"? By Ross's own candid admission, he has never seen a dinosaur (since he believes they became extinct 65+ million years ago; see pp. 48-49), thus he obviously never has observed every dinosaur that walked on land (or dinosaur-like reptile that swam in the oceans). As Dr. Henry Morris remarked in his book *The Biblical Basis for Modern Science,* "To say that the leviathan could not have breathed fire is to say much more than we know about leviathans (or water dragons or sea serpents)" (1984, p. 359, parenthetical item in orig.). The truth is, Ross and many others simply cannot fathom a real animal with the ability to produce fire and smoke. Is this reasonable?

Ross and others, it seems, have forgotten that all animals, including the dinosaurs, were designed and created by God on days five and six of Creation. From the creationist's perspective, if Jehovah wanted to create one or more dinosaurs that could expel fire, smoke, or some deadly chemical out of their mouths without harming themselves, He certainly **could** have done so. Bearing in mind the way in which **God** described leviathan to Job in Job 41:18-21, and considering that many secular stories have circulated for millennia that describe "fiery dragons," it is logical to conclude that He **did** create such creatures. It seems fitting to ask doubters the same rhetorical question God asked Abraham long ago: "Is anything too hard for the Lord?" (Genesis 18:14). Who is Hugh Ross (or anyone) to say that "no dinosaur...ever breathed fire"? The prophet Jeremiah proclaimed: "Ah, Lord God! Behold, You have made the heavens and the earth by Your great power and outstretched arm. **There is nothing too hard for You**" (32:17, emp. added).

What's more, even modern science gives us a glimpse into the likelihood of an animal being able to do something as impressive as breathe fire. When a person considers that an electric eel can produce enough electricity to stun a horse without ever shocking itself, that fireflies can make bioluminescent light, and that the Komodo dragon can store deadly bacteria inside its mouth (which only harms its prey, and never itself), it should be easy to accept the possibility that a dinosaur or a dinosaur-like reptile was capable of expelling certain hot, gaseous fumes that could ignite. Perhaps the closest living comparison to an extinct, fire-breathing animal is the little insect we call the bombardier beetle. One European encyclopedia described this creature as a "[b]eetle that emits an evil-smelling fluid from its abdomen, as a defence mechanism. This fluid rapidly evaporates into a gas, which appears like a minute jet of smoke, when in contact with air, and blinds the predator about to attack" ("Bombardier Beetle," 2007). In 1985, *TIME* magazine featured this amazing creature, calling its defense system "extraordinarily intricate, a cross between tear gas and a tommy gun" (Angier, 1985, p. 70). How can one look at a living bombardier beetle that produces a boiling

Electric eel
by Thomas Tarpley

Bombardier beetle

Used with permission from
Dr. Thomas Eisner

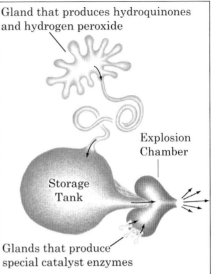

Gland that produces hydroquinones
and hydrogen peroxide

Explosion
Chamber

Storage
Tank

Glands that produce
special catalyst enzymes

Drawing by Thomas Tarpley

hot, acidic, noxious spray in its abdomen, which the insect
then expels from its back end in a rapid-fire action, and
conclude that no animal ever breathed fire or smoke?

In reality, whether a person is a creationist or an evolutionist,
he should have no problem believing in the possibility of
an animal breathing fire. Surely creationists believe that an
omniscient, omnipotent God **could** create a creature that
expels fire from its body. And, if evolutionists believe (1) that
the entire Universe came from the explosion of a period-size,
dense ball of matter 15 billion years ago, (2) that life came
from non-life, and (3) that the bombardier beetle evolved
the capability to shoot a 212-degree, noxious spray from its
back end, then they should think that an animal evolving
the ability to expel blasts of fire from its mouth would by no
means be implausible.

43

CONCLUSION

Evolutionist Mark Norell admitted that "all the mythical creatures…have real underpinnings in biology" (as quoted in Hajela, 2007). What real animals prompted dragon legends? What **rational** explanation exists for the multitude of dragon legends around the world? Why did peoples in different places and times, separated by thousands of miles, all come up with stories of giant reptiles that sound more like extinct dinosaurs than any other animal on Earth? Why are descriptions of dinosaur-like aquatic, aerial, and terrestrial animals given in reputable, historical writings, including the Bible? Why does history record the existence of large reptilian creatures with serpentine necks, elongated bodies, enormous tails, hard skin, stout legs, spiked backs, knobby heads, terrible teeth, snake-like tongues, horned or crested heads, sharp claws, and membranous wings? Why are the physical characteristics of many dragons so similar to the anatomy of various dinosaurs? Is all of this just a coincidence?

Unfortunately, those who continue to sympathize with evolutionists' billion-year timetable simply will not allow themselves to believe there actually is a connection between dinosaurs and dragons, even though it is readily apparent. Daniel Cohen admitted, "No creature that ever lived looked more like dragons than dinosaurs" (1975, p. 104). Yet, he went on to point out that since dinosaur fossils are supposedly millions of years old, "**we have to assume** that dinosaurs died out long before anyone could remember them…. [W]e **must assume** that dinosaurs have nothing to do with dragons" (pp.

106-107, emp. added). In truth, the problem is not with dragon legends and dinosaurs, but with the assumption-based, faulty dating methods of evolutionists (see DeYoung, 2005).

The reasonable view is that humans and dinosaurs once lived together, and the stories of their interaction were passed down from generation to generation. When you think about it, this is exactly what we would expect to find (ubiquitous stories of "dragons"), if humans once lived with dinosaurs.

Although there are other powerful evidences of the one-time coexistence of dinosaurs and humans (as will be discussed in chapters 4, 5, and 6), dragon legends certainly bear witness to the fact that dinosaurs and humans once lived together. Truly, evolutionists cannot logically explain away these historical "dinosaur descriptions."

> For since the creation of the world His invisible attributes are clearly seen, being understood by the things that are made, even His eternal power and Godhead, so that they are without excuse, because, although they knew God, they did not glorify Him as God, nor were thankful, but became futile in their thoughts, and their foolish hearts were darkened. **Professing to be wise, they became fools** (Romans 1:20-22, emp. added).

CHAPTER 4

Physical Evidence for the Coexistence of Dinosaurs and Humans—Part 1

People generally enjoy showing pictures of places they have visited and things they have seen. Simply telling someone about a trip, say to Sequoia National Park, is one thing; showing that person a picture of you standing next to the largest tree in Sequoia National Park, named General Sherman (which also is the largest tree on the planet), is entirely different. As the old adage goes, "a picture is worth a thousand words." People constantly take pictures of things they want to share with others. Someone on a safari in Africa may bring home pictures of an elephant he saw in the wild. Visitors to the

47

islands of Indonesia delight in showing pictures they took of real komodo dragons scurrying across the ground and up trees. Tourists in Alaska often are seen on roadsides capturing moose, doll sheep, and even grizzly bears on camera. Why? There are several reasons, but for many people it is to show others what they have seen. Pictures also authenticate the stories we tell.

Humans not only have told stories about large reptilian creatures (i.e., dragons/dinosaurs) for millennia (see chapters 2 and 3), the ancients also left behind "pictures" of these animals: some with serpentine necks, stout legs, elongated bodies, and enormous tails; others with knobby heads, short necks, plated backs, and spiked tails. Of course, these pictures are not the kind we take today, but paintings and carvings on rocks, in caves, on pottery, etc. Like the deer, goats, monkeys, mammoths, and other animals that have been discovered around the world carved or painted on rock walls by the ancients, various ancient "pictures" of dinosaurs have also been uncovered. If humans really did coexist with these animals at one time, such pictures are exactly what one would expect to find.

Ancient Cambodian Temple

THE *STEGOSAURUS* OF CAMBODIA

The Khmer civilization once flourished in the Southeast Asian territory of Angkor. Hindu and Buddhist kings during the 8th through 13th centuries A.D. built majestic stone temples

Bible.ca

throughout the area (NOTE: Information about the Khmer civilization, its rulers, and temples is derived from Freeman and Jacques, 1999, unless otherwise noted). In approximately 1186, King Jayavarman VII undertook the building of Ta Prohm, a stone monastery/temple. The Ta Prohm, which stands today in the overgrown jungles of Cambodia, was chosen by one of the major preservation societies "to be left in its 'natural state,' as an example of how most of Angkor

49

Bible.ca

looked on its discovery in the 19th century" (p. 136).

Intricately carved statues and stone columns fill the temple-monastery. On the stones, the ancients depicted animals, people, gods, various plants, and a host of other decorative images. But one column of carvings maintains a special interest to those interested in dinosaur/human coexistence. Concerning this particular column, Freeman and Jacques wrote: "On the angles and corners of the porch are numerous small scenes and representations of animals, both real and mythical" (p. 144). Of special note, the authors wrote about one of the carved animals, saying: "Among the vertical strip of roundels in the angle between the south wall of the porch and the east wall of the main body of the *gopura* there is even **a very convincing representation of a stegosaur**" (p. 144, emp. added). In their other book on Angkor, Jacques and Freeman were even more emphatic, saying that the animal "bears a **striking resemblance** to a stegosaurus" (1997, p. 213 emp. added).

The credentials of both Claude Jacques and Michael Freeman are worth noting. The back cover text of *Ancient Angkor* states: "The renowned French scholar, Claude Jacques, has studied

Angkor and its history for the past 30 years." The inside front-flap further mentions that Jacques

> lived in Cambodia for nine years where he taught Khmer history at the Archaeology Department of Phnom Penh and pursued his research into Khmer civilization. He has been the Director of Studies at the Ecole Pratiques des Hautes Etudes for the last two decades, teaching the history of Southeast Asia. He is an expert in Sanskrit, Khmer and Cham scripts and is closely involved in the various restoration projects being [sic] at Angkor (1999).

Concerning Michael Freeman, the front cover flap notes that he

> has been photographing Southeast Asia intensively for twenty years, and Angkor for ten, producing many books on the art history and architecture of the region.... He is also the author of the *Guide to Khmer Temples in Thailand and Laos*, and was the first photographer to have prolonged access to Angkor after the country's two decades of war, genocide and civil war (1999).

In short, it would be extremely difficult to find two men more qualified to speak on the *Stegosaurus* carving at Ta Prohm. Of major significance is the fact that the authors view the carving as authentic, with absolutely no hint of forgery surrounding it.

The authenticity of the carving is virtually

undisputed. Don Patton made a trip to Ta Prohm in 2006 for the express purpose of seeing the carving. Patton listed several compelling reasons that effectively eliminate the idea of forgery. He wrote concerning the carving:

Bible.ca

1. Patina is still obvious in the recesses.

2. The depth of relief on the carvings that cover every square inch of this column, is more than half an inch. Removing the imagined "original" carving would have left a recessed surface. Then, carving the stegosaur on the recessed surface would require still deeper recesses. The above photograph clearly demonstrates that the carving is not recessed. It is flush with the other carvings. Since the plates on the back of the stegosaur protrude from the recessed background at least half an inch, it would not be possible to add them to the background by subsequent carving. The plates are an integral part of the rock surrounded by a recessed, patina covered background.

3. There is approximately 40 feet of overburden that would have been displaced in order to replace the entire block.

4. The blocks are held together, not with mortar, but with iron "staples" in the shape of a capital "**I**" typically about 8 inches long, 1.5 inches wide and 3/8 of an inch thick. An inset in the shape of the staple was carved into the surface

of two adjoining blocks, across the abutment, one end in one block and the other end in the other. With the staple in the shaped recess, the next tier of blocks holds the staple in place. They are used horizontally and vertically…. However, the point that we are making here is that the blocks are interlocked in such a way that removing and replacing a block with 40 feet of overburden without detection, is an imaginary idea that will not work (Patton, 2006).

The primary objection, then, that this carving does not depict an actual *Stegosaurus* is not that it is a fake, but that the creature it depicts is not a *Stegosaurus*. Joseph Meert, in his blog dedicated to "refuting" young-Earth creationism, commented about the carving: "I thought it was a wild boar" (2007). He further commented: "The problem with the carving is that it does not really look like any modern or fossilized animal. That makes

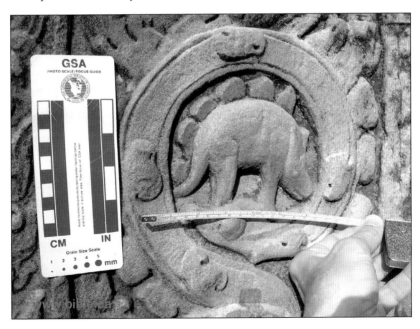

it more likely that it was some drug induced illusion (sort of like the rest of young earth creationist ideas!)" (2007). Another skeptical author wrote: "Could it be that the so-called plates are in fact just a decorative tree or a bush-type embellishment (the trunk is located underneath between the front and hind legs) located right behind the creature and nothing else? Could be!" ("The Stegosaurus Carving…," 2007).

The *prima facie* fallacy of these kinds of objections is the simple fact that the carving does not look like a wild boar or a decorative tree, but does, in fact, look **very** similar to a *Stegosaurus*. A class of third graders could easily attest to that fact. In reality, it takes a massive amount of creative imagination to make the carving look like something other than a *Stegosaurus*. After showing a picture of this carving to a middle school class for the first time, all 10 of the students in the class identified the animal as a dinosaur or specifically a *Stegosaurus*. Why is the carving even posted on the Internet if it looks like nothing more than a wild boar or a creature with bushes behind it? That the carving is posted and being discussed at length verifies that there is something extremely unique about it.

On closer inspection of the carving's head, it admittedly does not look exactly like the head of modern depictions of *Stegosauruses*–which is the primary objection to the idea that it is a *Stegosaurus*. Don Patton summarized this skeptical view:

> A few skeptics have based their objections on anatomical differences between popular Stegosaurus restorations and the Cambodian sculpture. The fact

that the average Jr. High student immediately identifies the sculpture as a Stegosaurus is considered of no consequence. 'The head is too large. Stegosaurs had no horns or frills on the head.' The sculpture has no spikes on the tail... Therefore, they conclude that the sculptor never saw a Stegosaurus (2006).

Patton refutes this view using a convincing line of reasoning. The view assumes that the modern anatomical ideas regarding the *Stegosaurus* are exactly right, with no room for variation. Patton wrote: "One is tempted to respond to these claims by pointing out that our modern restorations involve some guess work, that Stegosaurs may have exhibited a significant amount of anatomical variety (like dogs), that a view of tail spikes may well be blocked by the surrounding stone circle, etc., etc." (2006). Indeed, if modern science's study of dinosaurs has brought to light anything, it has revealed that some of our most cherished and commonly held images and ideas concerning dinosaur anatomy have been egregiously incorrect. For instance, in 1992 Stephen Czerkas wrote:

> Recent discovery of fossilized sauropod (diplodocid) skin impressions reveals a **significantly different** appearance for these dinosaurs. The fossilized skin demonstrates that a median row of [dermal] spines was present.... Some are quite narrow, and others are broader and more conical (1992, 20:1068, emp. added).

In an article titled "Rediscovering the Dinosaurs," Ned Potter noted that "Pittsburgh's Carnegie Museum of Natural History has one of the world's leading collections of dinosaur fossils" (2007). The newsworthy event pertaining to this huge dinosaur fossil collection is the fact that "the Carnegie staff has decided to dismantle—and rethink—its entire collection" (2007). Because of the rapid rate at which new fossils force paleontologists and museum curators to alter their old ideas, it is becoming evident that entire dinosaur collections have been pieced together incorrectly. Experts interviewed for the article noted that dinosaur bones "don't come with instruction manuals." "When the Carnegie museum in Pittsburgh opens its new dinosaur wing later this year, the skeletons will be posed as scientists **believe they would have looked** eons ago" (2007, emp. added). Admittedly, however, "[Y]ears from now, as scientists **learn more**, they say they'll probably have **to change the exhibit all over again**" (emp. added).

In truth, modern ideas about dinosaurs are adjusted every day, based on new fossil information. Add to that the fact that

dinosaur fossils are not as abundant as is commonly believed. For instance, Peter Dodson wrote an article titled, "Counting Dinosaurs: How Many Kinds Were There?," in which he made some very interesting observations. He stated:

> 45.3% of the dinosaur genera are represented by only a single specimen, and 74.0% have five specimens or fewer. Only 20.3% are based on essentially complete skulls and skeletons, and 56.8% include complete or partial skulls. Limited material often makes the

convincing definition of variational biological species difficult (1990, 87:7608).

Dodson explained that many of the dinosaurs we commonly see on movies or in magazines are constructed from very scant fossil remains. In regard specifically to *Stegosaurus* fossils, Dodson lists the top ten dinosaurs with the most articulated specimens found of their kind–of which *Stegosaurus* is not one. He listed the 10th place dinosaur as having 40 specimens available, which would mean that the *Stegosaurus* is represented by fewer specimens than that.

So, how many *Stegosaurus* skulls have been found? Finding the actual number is increasingly difficult. Various scholarly books, articles, and journals have little or nothing to say about the number of fossils available for each kind of dinosaur. After making a personal call to the American Museum of Natural History, a researcher from the Fossil Amphibian, Reptile, and Bird Collections division sent an e-mail with his results, in which he stated: "Only three complete *Stegosaurus* skulls are known. Additionally there are four almost complete skulls of *Hesperosaurus* thought to be referable to *Stegosaurus* as the skulls are indistinguishable. There are also 24 other incomplete skull specimens" (2007). Thus, it seems there are only three complete skulls and 28 partial skulls, many of which could be composed of only a few fragments of jawbone or teeth. When one considers the numerous replicas of *Stegosaurus* in museums all over the world, such limited numbers of complete fossilized skulls do not elicit total confidence in our present-day anatomical knowledge of *Stegosaurus*. Could it be that certain species of stegosaurs not represented by the few extant skulls had larger heads like the one in the carving?

There exists another, probably more likely, explanation regarding the carving's appearance. Patton commented: "The relevant question is not, Can you find anatomical differences with today's popular restorations? Rather, the real question is, What kind of sculpture would be produced by an artist who remembered seeing a *Stegosaurus*?" (2006). He further commented: "Assuming the sculptor did not have a *Stegosaurus* trained to pose as a model, and there was no access to the internet, the rendering would most likely be from memory. Would the results of this process necessarily be anatomically correct compared to today's restorations? What would it look like?" (2006).

To determine what a person familiar with *Stegosaurus* anatomy might draw from memory, Patton asked an art professor at the University of Texas at Arlington to have an art class draw a *Stegosaurus* from memory. Out of the 36 drawings from as many students, Patton posted 12 on his Web site for comparison to the carving. Patton then stated: "I think you will agree with the instructor's assessment that none of the students' efforts

looked as good as the sculpture on the temple wall in Cambodia" (2006). In actuality, the carving looks like what you would expect a person to carve who might have been working from memory. In addition, the ancient Cambodian artist had a limited circular area with which to work, and was forced to confine the sculpture to that small circle. Such physical constraints would certainly play a part in the "perfect" anatomical accuracy that could be rendered in the given area. Consider the picture below of a toy dinosaur that was originally (when sold) confined within a toy dinosaur egg. Toy makers made the easily identifiable *Stegosaurus* without tail spikes. This particular feature of the dinosaur was purposefully left off of the toy model for various reasons (e.g., space limitation within the egg), yet any child remotely familiar with dinosaurs knows that toy makers were intending to manufacture a *Stegosaurus.* This realization takes us back to the fact that, regardless of whether the Cambodia carving was anatomically accurate, practically any class of third-graders

across the country would identify the creature as a *Stegosaurus.* The simple truth is, the unmistakable carving of a dinosaur at the Ta Prohm temple near Siem Reap, Cambodia, testifies to the one-time cohabitation of dinosaurs and humans.

Bible.ca

ANOTHER OBJECTION CONSIDERED

Before we leave this particular carving, we need to consider another common objection to the idea that carvings that look like dinosaurs represent real creatures. Those who insist that dinosaurs and humans did not live together claim that the animals depicted in ancient art that look like dinosaurs are imaginary creatures that have no basis in reality. These people suggest that since we know carvings of imaginary gods, minotaurs, mermaids, and aliens have no basis in reality, neither should we think that dinosaur-like creatures do–regardless of how much they may resemble dinosaurs. John Clayton wrote:

> Finding an ancient picture of a dragon, minotaur, or alien-looking creature and assuming it is in reality what people saw is an **incredibly ignorant thing to do**. This applies to creationists who try to maintain people of 4,000 years ago cavorted with dinosaurs, but also to atheists who attempt to explain the origin of life by claiming

aliens seeded the planet with DNA packets. There is no evidence for either of these proposals, and neither of them has any historical support (2007, 34[4]:4. emp. added).

A major problem arises, however, when those such as Clayton attempt to lump "dragons" in with other creatures such as minotaurs or aliens. No physical evidence is available to verify the existence of the minotaur. Furthermore, the laws of biology preclude even the possibility of such. We do not believe the ancients saw minotaurs **because we do not believe there ever were minotaurs**. The situation with creatures that look like dinosaurs is much different. Everyone involved in the discussion believes that huge reptiles once roamed the Earth. The question is not "did huge reptilian creatures that match the ancient carvings exist?" The question is, "did they exist **with**

"The Minotaur"
George Frederick Watts
1885

61

humans?" Dinosaurs are not imaginary creatures dismissed by reputable sources. Their bones have been found, fossilized nests uncovered, and their skin impressions studied. Millions of dollars every year pour into dinosaur research. If thousands of minotaur fossils had been found, some of them very close to the carvings that depict creatures that looked just like minotaurs, we could not dismiss minotaurs as imaginary creatures, and the carvings and drawings could not be dismissed as depictions of imaginary creatures. The difference between art depicting minotaurs and art showing dinosaur-like creatures is that everyone knows dinosaurs existed—a fact not up for debate.

We have fossil evidence for *Dracorex*, but none for minotaurs.

THE LONGNECK OF ENGLAND

Another interesting dinosaur engraving lies in the floor of the Carlisle Cathedral in Carlisle, England. Founded in the 12th century, the Carlisle Cathedral has served as a meeting place for the people of northwest England for 900 years. One of the bishops of Carlisle in the 15th century was Richard Bell. He served in this position for 17 years, resigned in 1495, and died one year later (see Pryde, et al., 1996, p. 236). Bell's body was then laid to rest in a tomb along a main aisle inside the cathedral. His tomb is inlaid with brass and currently is covered by a protective rug in order to preserve the brass engravings as much as possible. In 2002, the Canon Warden of the cathedral removed the rug in order for United Kingdom resident Philip Bell (apparently no relation to Richard Bell) to examine the tomb.

Image courtesy of CreationOnTheWeb.com

63

According to Bell:

> The brass shows Bishop Richard Bell (1.44 m or 4 ft 8½ inches long) under a Gothic canopy (2.9 m or 9 ft 5 in long), dressed in his full vestments, with his mitre (bishop's cap) and crosier (hooked staff).

> But it is the narrow brass fillet (2.9 m or 9½ ft long), running around the edge of the tomb, that contains the items of particular interest. Owing to the passage of time (and countless thousands of tramping feet!) parts of the fillet have long since been lost, including the entire bottom section. However, in between the words of the Latin inscription, there are depictions of various…fish, an eel, a dog, a pig, a bird… (2003, 25[4]:40).

Most remarkable, however, is an engraving of two animals with long necks and long tails. Although some of the brass

Image courtesy of Enlightened.org.uk

engraving is worn due to 500 years of wear and tear, these curious creatures are clearly of some extinct animal. In truth, more than any other creature, they resemble the sauropod dinosaurs that once roamed the Earth.

What do critics have to say about the engravings? After passing off the animal on the left as "some kind of big cat," one popular skeptical Web site admitted: "The animal to the right, though, does look rather more like a quadrupedal dinosaur than any other sort of animal, past or present" ("Bishop Bell's…," 2007). What's more, the skeptics acknowledged the

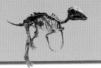

unlikelihood of the engraving being a hoax: "In the case of Bishop Bell's dinosaur, there is no corresponding profit motive, or any other apparent motive; and also, any tampering with the tomb would have to be done *in situ*, in Carlisle Cathedral, and it is hard to see how a hoaxer could have gone about his work unobserved" ("Bishop Bell's...").

It seems clear, even to skeptics, that at least one of the two curious engravings looks like a dinosaur. What is so spectacular about a dinosaur being engraved on a tomb built in 1496? Simply that the engraving is more than 300 years older than the first dinosaur fossils found in modern times. We have no evidence of humans finding dinosaur fossils and reconstructing their skeletons until the middle of the 19th century. So how did someone engrave such a convincing picture of a dinosaur in the late 15th century? The obvious, but often rejected answer, is men once lived with these creatures, and proof of their coexistence is found all over the world in the form of physical, historical, and biblical evidence. Thus, evolution's multi-million-year-dinosaur timetable is wrong.

Image courtesy of CreationOnTheWeb.com

THE *APATOSAURUS* OF SOUTHEASTERN UTAH

On the underside of the third largest natural bridge in the world (Kachina Bridge), several petroglyphs and pictographs exist, which rock-art experts believe to be anywhere from 500 to 1,500 years old. The carvings are believed to be the work of the Anasazi Indians who once lived in that area of southeastern Utah. A mountain goat, a human figure, multiple handprints, and many other carvings and drawings can be seen quite easily underneath the bridge on both sides of the span. The most fascinating piece of rock art at Kachina Bridge, however, is the petroglyph of a dinosaur, located to the right of the span, about 10 feet from the ground. This figure, which is carved into the rock, has a long, thick tail, a long neck, a wide

Kyle at the Natural Bridges National Monument entrance

Kachina Bridge

midsection, and a small head. Any unbiased visitor to Kachina Bridge would have to admit that this particular petroglyph looks like a dinosaur–specifically *Apatosaurus* (more popularly known as *Brontosaurus*).

In May of 2004, after examining this petroglyph firsthand and taking many pictures of it, as well as of the surrounding rock art, we visited the Natural Bridges National Monument visitor's center where we spoke with one of the staff members. Upon informing the Natural Bridges assistant that we had just hiked down to the base of Kachina Bridge, she immediately asked if we saw the petroglyph that resembles a dinosaur. We acknowledged that we had, and then asked her how "they" explain such an anomaly? (If, according to evolutionary scientists, humans never lived with dinosaurs, how did the Anasazis, who inhabited

Images of some of the petroglyphs found on the Kachina Bridge: hand prints (top), man (bottom left), and a wild goat (bottom right).

southeastern Utah from A.D. 500 to 1450, carve such an accurate picture of an *Apatosaurus* onto the side of a rock wall?) Her response: "They don't really want to explain it." After being politely pressed for more information, she indicated that the petroglyph was carved too early to be a horse, because the Anasazis did not have horses. She also commented that some people actually think it really is a picture of a dinosaur, but "they are crazy." She further explained that there are petroglyphs that resemble mammoths

Color has been enhanced in this photo of the Natural Bridges petroglyph to show the dinosaur shape more clearly.

around this area. So the petroglyph at Kachina Bridge may be just "some monster" that the Anasazis carved onto rock.

The only other animal that the staff member at Natural Bridges National Monument seemed to think that the petroglyph in question could have been was a horse. But, according to her own testimony, the Anasazi Indians were a horseless people. (Spanish settlers did not introduce the horse to America until the 16th century.) Thus, she concluded the petroglyph is simply some kind of monster. This "monster," however, looks exactly like the scientific reconstruction of the large sauropod dinosaur known as *Apatosaurus*. It is no wonder that this woman earlier admitted that scientists "don't really want to explain" this petroglyph. They do not want to deal with it, because they cannot find a logical way to explain it.

Interestingly, no one with whom we spoke about the petroglyph, nor any reputable writer whose works we have consulted on the matter, has challenged the authenticity of the petroglyph. In fact, two well-known rock-art experts have written about this particular petroglyph, and neither has suggested that it is a modern-day forgery. Francis Barnes, an evolutionist and widely recognized authority on rock art of the American Southwest, observed in 1979: "There is a petroglyph in Natural Bridges National Monument that bears **a startling resemblance to a dinosaur**, specifically a Brontosaurus, with long tail and neck, small head and all" (Barnes and Pendleton, 1979, p. 201, emp. added). Barnes also pointed out that other animals, such as impalas, ostriches, and mammoths, are seen on rock-art panels in the Southwest, that either have been long extinct in the Western Hemisphere or were thought to have never been there at all. "Such anomalous rock art figures can be explained away," wrote Barnes, "but they still tend to cast doubt upon the admittedly flimsy relative-time age-dating schemes used by archaeologists" (p. 202). More than 20 years

Apatosaurus

later, evolutionary geologist Dennis Slifer wrote about this petroglyph in his *Guide to Rock Art of the Utah Region.*

> At the base of Kachina Bridge are approximately one hundred elements, both petroglyphs and pictographs, dating from A.D. 700-1250. These include a series of red handprints and a large red butterfly-like figure, spirals, bighorn sheep, snake-like meandering lines, a white pictograph of a chain-like design, and some geometric petroglyphs.... One of the most curious designs is **a petroglyph that resembles a dinosaur**, which is apparently of Anasazi origin based on its patination (2000, p. 105, emp. added).

Following these comments, Slifer included a diagram of the petroglyph in question—the illustration looks exactly like a dinosaur (specifically, some kind of large sauropod).

An illustration similar to the one in Slifer's book of the Natural Bridges "petroglyph that resembles a dinosaur."

Both Barnes and Slifer know that the dinosaur petroglyph at Natural Bridges National Monument shows every sign of age. One can be sure that, if there were any orthodox way to explain it away, they would have attempted to do so. In fact, earlier in his book, Slifer did not hesitate to state his systematic objections to another particular piece of rock art that some have asserted is a pictograph of an extinct pterosaur (see pp. 59-63). The petroglyph at Kachina Bridge, however, was not, and could not, be explained away in any logical fashion.

THE DINOSAUR MUSEUM

What could further verify that this particular petroglyph depicts an actual dinosaur seen by the Anasazi Indians? How about *Apatosaurus* fossils in the surrounding area? If apatosaurs had ever lived in the area, then that would lend credence to the idea that the Anasazis had seen them. Interestingly, just 45 miles from Natural Bridges National Monument, in Blanding, Utah, two actual *Apatosaurus* hip fossils are displayed. The bones were found in the 1960s **in the**

Eric stands beside *Apatosaurus* hip fossils in Blanding, Utah.

Blanding area—less than 50 miles from the *Apatosaurus*-like petroglyph at Natural Bridges National Monument. An ancient petroglyph that looks just like an *Apatosaurus*, with bones from the very same type of animal, found within 50 miles of the carving. Taken together, this type of evidence presents an impressive case for the coexistence of dinosaurs and humans.

71

THE DINOSAUR OF NORTHERN ARIZONA

On two occasions in the late 1800s, Dr. Samuel Hubbard, Honorary Curator of Archaeology of the Oakland Museum, visited an area of the Grand Canyon known as the Havasupai Canyon. Hubbard observed many curious inscriptions on the canyon walls during these trips. Though the significance of the pictographs and petroglyphs was not fully recognized early on, "[e]ndeavors were made at various times to interest scientists" to view the artwork (Hubbard, 1925, p. 5). Finally, in the fall of 1924, Hubbard, a theistic evolutionist (cf. pp. 37-38), made his third trip to Havasupai, this time accompanied by several men, including renowned paleontologist Charles W. Gilmore, photographer Robert Carson, and the oil tycoon who sponsored the expedition, E.L. Doheny.

Hubbard was not merely impressed with the fact that the ancients drew and carved images on rock, or that "they show every sign of a great antiquity" (1925, p. 7). Indeed, "'[d]esert

The Doheny Scientific Expedition
"Hitting the Trail"

varnish' *had commenced to form* in the cut" of the petroglyphs, "indicating an unbelievable antiquity" (p. 9, italics in orig.). More than anything else, Hubbard was amazed by the **kind** of animals the ancients carved. According to Hubbard, "*no ibex*, not even fossil ones, have ever been found in America" (p. 17, emp. in orig.), yet in three different

Members of Samuel Hubbard's team taking pictures at the Grand Canyon

places in the Havasupai Canyon, the team discovered ibex inscriptions. Hubbard noted:

> Supplementing the pictures of ibex from the Supai Canyon…I have received other ibex pictures from Nevada, Oregon, Utah and Arizona. I am therefore forced to the conclusion that this must have been a very common animal at one time inhabiting the whole Rocky Mountain region. It was probably such a favorite game of the prehistoric hunters that they finally exterminated it (p. 27).

Indeed, "[t]hese drawings would seem to indicate that they must have been a common animal in the Grand Canyon region" in the distant past (p. 17). After all, how could the ancients have inscribed such accurate pictures of them, if they had never seen them?

On one particular rock wall in the Havasupai Canyon, just above a group of ibex inscriptions, is a carving of an

73

elephant. "The remains of elephants are very common all over North America"—from Alaska to Mexico (Hubbard, 1925, p. 15). Furthermore, as noted earlier in our discussion of the Natural Bridges rock art, inscriptions that resemble elephants or mammoths are not unusual in the West. Undoubtedly, elephants once roamed North America. Consider, however, the implications of elephant and mammoth rock art. For the ancients to have drawn images of these massive creatures with long trunks, it is reasonable to conclude that, as with the ibex, Native Americans must have seen elephants. Interestingly, the inscriptions at Havasupai show an elephant striking a man with its trunk (see Hubbard, 1925, pp. 12-13; see also Hubbard, 1926, 26[35]:13).

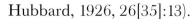

Although ancient **American** elephant and ibex rock art is fascinating in and of itself, as is the American rhinoceros carved on a rock wall near Moab, Utah (Hubbard, 1925, p. 27), what caught Hubbard's attention more than anything else at Havasupai was a figure "cut into the sandstone much more deeply than the elephant" (p. 16). Its height was 11.2 inches, had a neck approximately 5.1 inches in length and a tail right at 9.1 inches. Hubbard photographed the petroglyph and eventually placed it in the scientific monograph he authored, titled *Discoveries Relating to Prehistoric Man by the Doheny Scientific*

Expedition in the Hava Supai Canyon (1925, p. 10). What kind of animal is it? What kind of animal had a long neck, long tail, wide body, and once roamed northern Arizona? Dr. Hubbard believed that he had found an ancient drawing of a dinosaur. He wrote:

> The fact that some prehistoric man made a pictograph of a dinosaur on the walls of this canyon upsets completely all of our theories regarding the antiquity of man.... The fact that the animal is upright and balanced on its tail would seem to indicate that the prehistoric artist must have seen it alive (pp. 5,7, emp. in orig.).

Evidence "that dinosaurs were in the vicinity, is proved by the tracks...which were identified by Mr. Gilmore [a vertebrate paleontologist and renowned dinosaur fossil hunter–EL/KB] as belonging to one of the carnivorous dinosaurs" (p. 9).

EDMONTOSAURUS

Image courtesy of Eden Communications

Bible.ca

According to Hubbard, "These tracks were in the 'Painted Desert' not over 100 miles from the picture" (p. 9).

Once again, we have a carving of an animal that looks more like a dinosaur than any other animal, living or extinct. What's more, all of the evidence points to the carving being genuine. Finally, fossil footprints prove that dinosaurs once lived in the same general area of the dinosaur-like rock art. Yet again, we ask: How could man have drawn such an accurate picture of a creature he supposedly never had seen? The fact is, man once lived with dinosaurs, and the carvings and engravings in Asia, Europe, and North America serve as strong evidence of their cohabitation.

CHAPTER 5

Physical Evidence for the Coexistence of Dinosaurs and Humans—Part 2

THE JULSRUD COLLECTION

The small, obscure town of Acambaro in the state of Guanajuato in Mexico houses one of the most unique antiquities collections in the world. In 1945, a German hardware merchant named Waldemar Julsrud happened across a half-buried clay figurine at the bottom of a mountain known as el Toro (the Bull). Julsrud was no stranger to artifacts of ancient civilizations. He owned one of the most valuable and extensive collections of Chupicuaro pottery in existence. Charles Hapgood noted: "Mr. Julsrud possesses at the present time one of the best

Waldemar Julsrud (on the left)

collections of this pottery (Tarascan–EL/KB) in existence, comprising several hundred pieces" (1955, 2:1). [NOTE: At the time, the pottery was believed to be Tarascan, but was later assigned to the pre-classical Chupicuaro culture (800 B.C. to A.D. 200) (see Swift, n.d.[a]).] But the newly discovered ceramic figurines did not match any ancient civilization with which Julsrud was familiar.

The ceramic figurines intrigued Julsrud, and he wanted to know if more were buried nearby. He made an arrangement with one of his employees, Odilon Tinajero, to dig in the area in an attempt to find more pieces. Julsrud agreed to pay Tinajero one peso for every figurine that was complete, or could be easily put back together. In all, Julsrud eventually collected over 33,500 figurines. The sheer number of figurines was enough to turn heads, but the fact that many of the figurines depicted

reptiles that closely resembled dinosaurs in direct contact and interaction with human figures was even more startling to the scientific community. Furthermore, the apparent antiquity of the find predated modern fossil discoveries by hundreds of years, so any accurate information regarding dinosaur anatomy would have necessarily been from the ancient civilization's interaction with the creatures.

Reports about the amazing find began to surface. Julsrud wrote a booklet titled *Enigmas del Pasado*, in which he gave specific details regarding the collection. After its publication, reporters began to contact him. Lowell Harmer, writer for the *Los Angeles Times*, visited Julsrud in Acambaro and wrote an article in the March 25, 1951 *Times*. He titled the article: "Mexico Finds Give Hint of Lost World: Dinosaur Statues Point to Men Who Lived in Age of Reptiles." Harmer mentioned the huge number of statues that had been found, saying that

Bible.ca

they "filled the floors, the tables, and the wall cabinets to overflowing" in Julsrud's house (1951, p. B1). Harmer further discussed the intricacy with which many of the figurines were crafted: "Most of the pottery pieces are elaborate masterpieces. Days of careful talented work went into many of the larger ceramics. How could it be a hoax? Not even in Mexico, where money is so scarce, could anyone afford the labor of these thousands of statues at the low prices Julsrud is paying" (1951, p. B1). Harmer seemed fairly convinced of the collection's authenticity, but concluded his article by saying, "I am a writer, not an archaeologist. It will be up to the experts to decide."

Bible.ca

A few months later, in 1952, William N. Russell made a trip to Acambaro and wrote about the amazing figurines. His article, "Did Man Tame the Dinosaur?" appeared in the February/March 1952 issue of *Fate* magazine. In that article, Russell mentioned that Julsrud had collected 26,000 pieces, which filled the rooms of Julsrud's house. Russell said that "[t]here were thousands upon thousands of the weird objects" (1952, 5[2]:23). From his observations, he concluded that there were no

duplicate pieces. "Each is either hand-molded, hand-carved or both," he said (5[2]:25). Russell stayed several days to interview Julsrud. He concluded with these words: "We cannot expect hurried pronouncements of authenticity. But, in my opinion, nothing should becloud the evidence that Julsrud's objects are very old" (5[2]:27).

The reports about the authenticity of the find would not go unchallenged. After all, if the collection was what it appeared to be, then the entire evolutionary scenario of human and dinosaur history would need to be rewritten to account for the accurate knowledge of dinosaur anatomy possessed by the ancient crafters of the Julsrud collection. Charles DiPeso, an archaeologist associated with the Amerind Foundation, decided to make a trip to Acambaro in an attempt to determine the authenticity of the collection. Several sample sherds of the collection had been sent to the Amerind Foundation for testing. Those at the Foundation did extensive chemical testing on the sherds. DiPeso wrote:

> Chemical tests were made of the soils composing the figurines. Sherds were crushed and the contents were inspected for any inclusions that might give a clue as to the date of manufacture. Laboratory tests proved nothing. It was therefore decided that a representative should be sent into the field to witness the actual excavation of the figurines (1953a, 18[4]:388).

It is interesting to note that the Amerind Foundation could not conclude that the sherds were recent fabrications from the chemical tests they performed.

DiPeso was chosen as the representative for the trip. DiPeso's biased attitude against the authenticity of the collection was evident from the beginning. He stated:

> The Amerind Foundation, Inc., was prevailed upon to make an investigation of the materials. To imply falsification merely on the strength of the life-forms represented was not sufficient, for there was **always the bare possibility** that the figurines were chance similarities to Mesozoic forms as defined by modern scientists in the last two hundred years. It was within the realm of chance that they were the work of some **imaginative** prehistoric artist who may have taken his inspiration from the **smaller reptiles still in existence today** (1953a, 18[4]:388, emp. added).

Notice the implications of DiPeso's statements. First, he approached the find with the idea that its authenticity was only a **bare** possibility. Then, he did not even consider the possibility that the ancient artist might have actually seen dinosaurs. He only admitted the chance that the ancient artist might have copied small, living reptiles and elaborated upon them.

Bible.ca

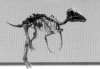
What would you expect someone with this kind of bias to conclude when he witnessed pieces in the collections that looked like known kinds of dinosaurs? Simply on the basis of his bias, he would be forced to deny the collection's authenticity.

It was no surprise, then, when DiPeso issued his report stating that the collection was a fraud. He gave several reasons that allegedly supported this conclusion. He wrote:

> Further, none of the specimens were marred by patination nor did they possess the surface coating of soluble salts…. The figures were broken, in most cases, where the appendages attached themselves to the body of the figurines…. No parts were missing. Furthermore, none of the broken surfaces were worn smooth. In the entire collection of 32,000 specimens no shovel, mattock, or pick marks were noted (1953a, 18[4]:388).

DiPeso also stated: "Further investigation revealed that a family living in the vicinity of Acambaro make these figurines during the winter months when their fields lie idle" (1953a, 18[4]:388). DiPeso further claimed that the hole from which he watched figurines being excavated showed signs of recent digging prior to the excavation and signs of figurine "planting." He concluded: "Thus the investigation ended: it seems almost superfluous to state that the Acambaro figurines are not prehistoric nor were they made by a prehistoric race who lived in association with Mesozoic reptiles" (18[4]:389).

83

Several suspicious aspects of DiPeso's trip troubled those who wanted honest answers about the figurines. First, DiPeso spent little more than two days for his entire investigation. He only watched a tiny fraction of the figures be excavated. Second, he claimed to have inspected the entire collection of over 32,000 pieces, but he was only in Julsrud's house for about four hours. Furthermore, he did not take time to learn the method used by the excavators. Nor did he attempt to locate an undisturbed site to excavate. His conclusions had every sign of a trumped-up, predetermined expedition designed to refute the collection from the start. It is ironic that DiPeso's "research" is used most often to refute the authenticity of the collection, yet every one of his points was dealt with satisfactorily soon after his report.

News about the collection and DiPeso's expedition reached a man named Charles Hapgood who was commissioned to investigate the find at length. Hapgood, professor of anthropology at the University of New Hampshire, was well-qualified to do such an investigation. He had studied handcrafts at length. In the 1940s, Hapgood began a nationwide promotion of handcrafts. Eventually, he presented information to President Roosevelt concerning handcraft protection. The President appointed a commission to prepare legislation concerning handcraft protection, of which Hapgood became the executive secretary (Hapgood, 1955, 2:1). Erle Stanley Gardner, author of the famous *Perry Mason* series, commenting about Hapgood, said:

Erle Stanley (left), Charles Hapgood
(Back Center), and Carlos Julsrud, son of Waldemar

Now, Professor Hapgood is an interesting individual. He is essentially fair-minded, well-balanced, and not given to hasty decisions…. Professor Hapgood had started out studying history; then he had specialized in history as it affected primitive man. He became an omnivorous student and an outstanding authority in his field. His name carried great weight. Today he is an authority on ancient civilizations (Gardner, 1969, p. 13).

Hapgood had the credentials to inspect the Julsrud collection.

Hapgood's initial report was published in December 1955, a very rare document that is extremely difficult to find. In it, he stated the reason for his investigation. Referring to DiPeso's expedition, Hapgood said: "The previous investigations, extremely limited in character (one lasted half a day and the

Charles Hapgood

other two days) have failed to prove anything. Their evidence is purely negative and entirely inconclusive" (1955, p. 3). In the report, Hapgood addressed each of DiPeso's contentions.

No Missing Pieces?

DiPeso stated: "The figures were broken, in most cases, where the appendages attached themselves to the body of the figurines.... No parts were missing." In response to the breaking of the pieces at their appendages, Hapgood noted: "But what would be more natural than for pieces to break at their weakest points?" (1955, 5:7). Furthermore, concerning the missing parts, he said: "As for missing parts, I have personally

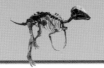

inspected a number of large boxes which are completely filled with parts of figurines that could not be put together because parts were found missing" (1955, 5:7). Hapgood's testimony coincides with that of other observers of the collection. William Russell said: "Julsrud showed me several figurines…. And there were **many hundreds of broken pieces** stacked in boxes" (1952, 5[2]:25, emp. added). Lowell Harmer, in his article in the *Los Angeles Times*, recounted his trip to Julsrud's house, in which he saw "a few wooden boxes of **unreassembled parts** of dinosaur pottery resting here and there on benches" (1951, emp. added). Harmer further told of how he and Julsrud visited the digging area, where "[h]undreds **of broken pieces of dinosaur statues** were still scattered among the rocks and the magueys" (1951, emp. added). Concerning broken and "missing" pieces of figurines, Erle Stanley Gardner, recounting his trip to el Toro mountain in Acambaro during the late 1960s, wrote: "Now here I was in for the surprise of my life because, as we spread out along the cut bank of the road, it became apparent that the soil was **literally filled with broken pieces** of pottery, obsidian knives, and here **and there a part of a figure**" (1969, p. 232, emp. added).

NO DIGGING MARKS ON FIGURINES?

Furthermore, DiPeso stated: "In the entire collection of 32,000 specimens no shovel, mattock, or pick marks were noted" (1953a, 18[4]:388). In response, Hapgood stated: "As nearly as I can learn, Mr. DiPeso spent not more than four hours in his inspection of this collection. I have examined it **many hours daily for several weeks**, and I cannot claim to have examined more than a small fraction of the objects. Yet **I have seen innumerable breaks** that could have been made by shovel or pick" (1955, 5:7, emp. added). Concerning DiPeso's claim, John Tierney wrote: "Amid a host of outrageously false or erroneous observations he made was the claim to have precisely examined every one of the then 32,000 artifacts to determine whether there were shovel marks, a feat which would have required inspection of 133 artifacts per minute steadily for four hours" (1994b, 1[4]:56). When Don Patton and Dennis Swift made a trip to Acambaro, they recounted how they were allowed to see several of the figurines. Swift wrote: "Working at a fast pace, in a six hour period, a little more than eight hundred

of the ceramic figurines were unwrapped" (Swift, n.d.[a]). In regard to DiPeso's claim, Swift correctly noted: "In reality, it would take several days to unpack the massive jumble of intact, broken, and repaired pieces from the boxes. Once the boxed pieces were disentangled and set up with those already on display in the mansion, it would take many more days to even give a cursory examination" (n.d.[a]). DiPeso simply could not have given the collection anything like a close examination in the time he spent.

Bible.ca

NO PATINA OR ENCRUSTED DIRT?

Another of DiPeso's pieces of "evidence" used to refute the find's authenticity was that the pieces did not have dirt or patina encrusting them. He said: "Further, none of the specimens were marred by patination nor did they possess the surface coating of soluble salts…" (1953a, 18[4]:388). Concerning this allegation, Hapgood responded: "I cannot understand why Mr. DiPeso did not find dirt in the crevices of the Julsrud figurines. I found very many figurines, which, despite their washing, still showed such dirt, and in the case of the musical instruments a majority could not be played because their interiors **were choked with dirt**" (1955, 5:6, emp. added). Swift and Patton commented: "In the process of handling several hundred pieces of the Julsrud collection, the authors have observed pieces that still have dirt embedded in the crevices as well as some patina on the surface" (Swift, n.d.[a]). This is, indeed, remarkable, since Julsrud paid one peso for every complete piece that was washed and cleaned. He did not know that removing patina and encrusted dirt from the figurines would cast doubt on their authenticity. Yet, for all the washing and cleaning that was done, dirt and patina were still evident.

DISTURBED EXCAVATION AREA?

DiPeso's main argument was that the site, from which the figurines he saw were excavated, looked as if it had already been disturbed. Hapgood countered with an explanation of the excavation procedure. He wrote: "An important point that came out was that when the digger stopped work in the middle of excavating a cache, he filled in the hole, to protect it from the many small boys of the neighborhood. This may have a bearing on the accusations of fraud..." (1955, 1:6). Not satisfied, however, to rely solely on this explanation, Hapgood determined to find an undisturbed area to see for himself. Concerning his activities on June 22, 1955, Hapgood wrote:

Bible.ca

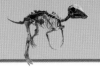

The next day we obtained permission to dig inside one of the houses erected on the site. This was owned by Acambaro's Chief of Police, Juan Mandujano. Since the general site had been so thoroughly searched by the digger over a period of about eight years, it seemed that the best possibility of finding a cache of figurines would be under one of the houses. 'Planting' of figurines in that case would also be difficult, if not impossible. So far as I could find out, the house was built about 25 years ago (1930–EL/KB). I found every part of the floor of the house smooth, and extremely hard. The diggers worked through the floor with picks, and I saw the hard layer was about eight inches thick. Under this was a somewhat softer layer of earth, which overlay the original sloping surface of the ground. The original surface was easily discernible in the stratification and was complete. There appeared to be no doubt that the original surface had not been disturbed since the fill was piled on it to level the floor when the house was built…. Below the original sloping surface were found many fragments of pots, and many fragments of figurines. All the figurine fragments were clearly typical of the Julsrud collection (1955, 1:2-3).

Hapgood, however, was not the only person who had successfully located the figurines at sites that were verified to be undisturbed. John Tierney noted:

In one of the most remarkable episodes in all archaeological history, an official team of four Mexican archaeologists, headed by Dr. Eduardo Noguera, Director of Prehispanic Monuments of the Instituto Nacional de Antropologia e Historia, supervised a dig at the Julsrud site in 1954. It admitted (contrary to the claims of DiPeso and Peterson) that the excavations were scientifically valid… (1994b, 1[4]:54).

Concerning this expedition, Hapgood noted:

> It seems to me significant that although other good observers have witnessed excavations, no one else has reported fraud. Among previous qualified witnesses were Dr. Raymond C. Barber, of the Los Angeles County Museum, and Dr. Eduardo Noguera. The former, to be sure is a minerologist [sic], although he is interested in archaeology, but Dr. Noguera is the director of Pre-hispanic monuments in Mexico. Dr. Noguera saw objects excavated and found no evidence of fraud in the burial; his [DiPeso's–EL/KB] subsequent conclusion that there must have been fraud was based entirely on his inability to explain the reptile forms (1955, 5:9).

[NOTE: Charles Hapgood mentioned that he found real teeth among the Julsrud collection. He stated: "I later took these teeth to Dr. George Gaylord Simpson, America's leading paleontologist, at the Museum of Natural History. He identified them as the teeth of *equus conversidans owen*, an extinct horse of the ice age" (2000, p. 82). The idea of extinct animals, such as dinosaurs, being depicted in the collections cannot be used to dismiss the collections.]

Suppose DiPeso did detect fraud. Although it is very doubtful, it would not account for the other excavations that were verified to be authentic by other experts. Furthermore, DiPeso found only about 50 figurines and pieces of pottery during his excavation. How could he discount the entire collection based on a cache of pieces that composed **.15%** (less than two tenths **of one percent**) of the collection?

A FABRICATING FAMILY?

Finally, DiPeso stated: "Further investigation revealed that a family living in the vicinity of Acambaro make these figurines during the winter months when their fields lie idle" (1953a, 18[4]:388). Several aspects of the collection prove this statement to be false.

Bible.ca

First, Julsrud paid the diggers one peso for every complete, cleaned piece he received. Yet, statements from Russell, Gardner, and Harmer verify that several thousand pieces were broken that Julsrud did not buy. Along these lines, Hapgood wrote:

> A significant point to me was that during our excavations the little boys (of whom there were sometimes as many as 17 clustered around us) would keep coming to us **with fragments** they had found at one time or another on the surface of the ground of the general site, and we would constantly be finding them ourselves. Inasmuch as it hardly seemed likely that anyone would make false figurines, age them, break them, and scatter them on the site to deceive us, I thought that these should be preserved as part of the evidence. These pieces are all typical of the

Julsrud collection, encrusted with dirt, many with rootlets or rootlet marks on them, and of two kinds of clay, black and red (1955, 1:4).

Second, many of the pieces were very intricate and would have taken an incredibly long time to make. Others were very large, some reaching lengths of five feet. Yet, Julsrud paid one peso for each piece, regardless of its intricacy or size. In describing a set of musical instruments found in the collection, Hapgood commented:

On more careful examination, a group of about sixty musical instruments in the Julsrud collection turned out to be most remarkable. No two were identical in shape. Many of them could still be blown, and had pure and beautiful tones. It was evident that there was a musical scale, the range from highest to lowest notes being very considerable, and the intervals of comparable value. Some instruments had several notes, one as many as eight (1955, 6:6).

Making a working musical instrument with eight notes would take much more time than sculpting a crude figure of a reptile. Why would a person take the time to add such detail when he only received a peso for each piece, regardless of its design?

Third, the size of the collection would have made it extremely difficult for one family to have perpetrated such a fraud. Alex

Pezzati concluded that the collection was not authentic, but nevertheless stated: "The sheer number of figurines seemed to make the possibility of faking them remote, unless an **entire crew of villagers** was involved. Also, if the aim was to hoodwink foreigners into buying fakes, one would expect the artifacts to resemble known types. Why fake such outlandish figures?" (2005, 47[3]:6-7). Erle Stanley Gardner assessed the situation as follows: "I don't believe that it would have been at all possible for any group of people to have made these figures, to have paid for the burro-load of wood necessary to 'fire' them, take them out and bury them, wait for the ground to resume its natural hardness which would take from one to ten years, and then 'discover' these figures and dig them up–all for a gross price of twelve cents per figure" (1969, p. 222). William Russell noted: "Julsrud's collection, if faked, would take literally centuries to produce unless hundreds of men and great amounts of money were involved" (1952, 5[2]:26). The amount of clay, wood required to bake the figurines, and hours needed to produce such a vast collection, simply could not have gone undetected. Nor would it have been a profitable venture at one peso per figurine. [NOTE: Julsrud did not make a habit of selling the figurines. Only a few times did he ever sell any of them. No one involved in the discussion has ever accused Julsrud of making the figurines or of selling them to make a profit. He merely collected and stored them, and would thus have no financial motivation to manufacture them himself or have them manufactured for monetary gain.]

Additionally, DiPeso claimed that the family of forgerers lived in the environs of Acambaro, but extensive investigation revealed that such simply could not be verified. Hapgood noted:

> The story of this ceramic family has been investigated, first by the municipal authorities, then by the Chamber of Commerce, then by Professor Ramon Rivera.... Both official bodies issued statements that no such family is known in Acambaro or the environs.... No trace of such a family was found by any of these people (1955, 5:9).

Dennis Swift wrote:

> Francisco Aguitar Sanchaz, Superintendent of the National Irrigation Plant of Solis said, "That on the basis of four years intimate knowledge of the inhabitants of the entire area and of archaeological activity there, he could positively deny that there was any such ceramic production in the vicinity." The Municipal President of Acambaro, Juan Terrazaz Carranza, issued on July 23, 1952, an official statement No. 1109 refuting Dipeso's allegation. "This Presidency under my direction ordered that an investigation be carried out in this matter, and has arrived at the

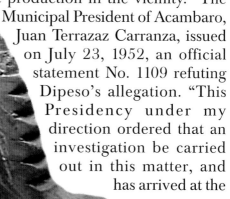

Bible.ca

conclusion that in this municipal area there does not exist any persons who makes these kinds of objects" (Swift, n.d.[a]).

DiPeso's allegation did not go uninvestigated, and the evidence suggesting that a family was responsible for forging the collections simply did not hold up. As Hapgood correctly summarized:

> It is clear that the scope of this alleged fraud is many times greater than that of any fraud ever perpetrated in the past. It would require an exceedingly great range of knowledge of Indian culture, and a not inconsiderable knowledge of paleontology. It would require also an inexhaustible power of imagination (for the objects are not imitations of known models) and an uncommon skill at sculpture (1955, 5:3).

No family in the area was ever discovered that possessed this kind of skill or knowledge.

THE CLINCHER

Perhaps the most powerful piece of evidence confirming the authenticity of the Julsrud collection is the knowledge of dinosaur anatomy present in the figurines, specifically one aspect of saurian anatomy that was unknown until the 1990s. Prior to the early 1990s, sauropod dinosaurs were constructed with smooth backs. The huge plant-eating dinosaurs such as *Diplodicus*, *Argentinasaurus*, and *Brachiosaurus* were believed to have no spikes on their backs, and were drawn without them in journals, books, magazines, etc. Yet, in a 1992 article, Stephen Czerkas wrote:

> Recent discovery of fossilized sauropod (diplodocid) skin impressions reveals a significantly different appearance

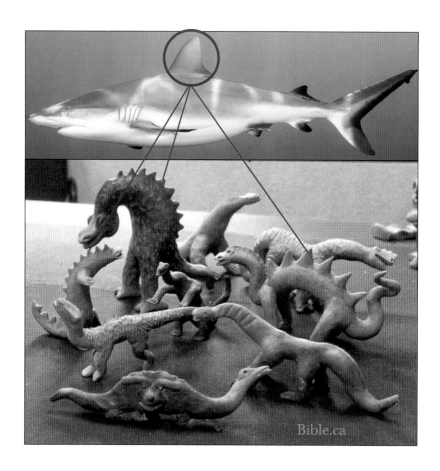

for these dinosaurs. The fossilized skin demonstrates **that a median row of [dermal] spines was present....** Some are quite narrow, and others are broader and more conical (1992, 20:1068, emp. added).

In 1992, it was discovered that sauropods had spines or spikes. The Julsrud collection was discovered between 1945-1953, over 40 years prior to Czerkas' discovery. If a person attempted to fake the figurines, he would not have put spines on the backs of sauropod dinosaurs. Yet, even a cursory inspection of photographs from the Julsrud collection shows that the sauropod dinosaurs

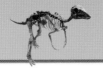
in the collection have spines. Pictures in Gardner's book show spiked sauropods in the collection, and his book was published in 1969, 23 years before the Czerkas' discovery (Gardner, 1969, pp. 9-11). Furthermore, the spikes on the sauropod figurines match the description of the ones found from recent skin impressions. Ellen Morris Bishop wrote: "The biggest spines found were about 9 inches long, shaped a little like a shark's dorsal fin. The smallest, at tail-tip, were about 3 inches high" (1993). The logical explanation as to how the Julsrud figurines possess accurate dinosaur anatomy unknown until 1992 is simply that the ancient artists who produced the figurines saw the dinosaurs and interacted with them in ways congruent with the figurine depictions.

Concerning the Julsrud collection, John Tierney correctly noted: "Nevertheless, the collection is a reality which threatens the orthodox concepts and time scales in many fields of study. It is no wonder there has been such determined opposition by dogma-bound academics" (1994a, 1[4]:16). When all the evidence is critically assessed, the Julsrud collection provides powerful evidence of the coexistence of humans and dinosaurs.

ICA STONES

Eugenia Cabrera is currently the Director of the Ica Stone Museum located in Ica, Peru. Her father, Dr. Javier Cabrera, starting in the 1930s, collected most of the 11,000 Ica stones that fill the museum she directs. The stones are controversial, to say the least. Depicted on the stones are what appear to be relics of an ancient Indian culture that predated the Incas. Many of the carved stones exhibit mundane scenes that would be expected in any ancient culture. But some of the carvings portray humans in close contact with dinosaurs. Scenes of men hunting dinosaurs, riding dinosaurs, and leading them by ropes around their necks present a glaring problem for the evolutionary scenario that humans and dinosaurs were separated by millions of years.

Because of the dinosaur carvings on the stones, the entire collection has been labeled a fraud by the evolutionary scientific community. Of course, that is exactly what would be expected, since the authentication of the stones would

Bible.ca

effectively annihilate decades of evolutionary propaganda as it relates to dinosaurs. Gainsayers of the stones present several lines of evidence that they believe debunks the stones. They say the carving on stones cannot be dated accurately because, while the stones could be dated using standard geological dating methods (which, by the way, are based on several

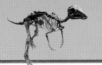

unprovable assumptions, see DeYoung, 2005), the carvings on the stones cannot be dated. Those who reject the authenticity of the stones also point to stones that have been faked and use them to discount the entire collection. Are the Ica stones frauds, or are they an amazing archaeological discovery that adds considerable evidence to the idea that humans lived with dinosaurs? A brief look at the salient points in the discussion reveals that the Ica stones are, in fact, authentic evidence for the co-existence of dinosaurs and humans.

OBJECTIONS CONSIDERED

Those who discount the stones have raised some serious objections to their authenticity. Each of those objections can be answered sufficiently to show that they do not militate against the genuineness of the stones.

The Carvings Cannot be Dated Using Standard Geological Dating Methods

While it is true that the carvings cannot be dated using standard geological dating methods, this fact does not disprove the stones' authenticity for several reasons. First, the standard geological dating methods are fraught with error. They often render results that are known to be incorrect by millions or billions of years (DeYoung, 2005). Furthermore, this line of reasoning would force archaeologists to reject all ancient carvings on any type of stone. Obviously, this is not how the study of ancient artifacts proceeds, so other considerations must be factored into the dating of any ancient carving. Other questions must also be considered: Where was the carving found? Does it exhibit knowledge of a culture or fauna that would be difficult for modern carvings to obtain? Does the carving show the wear of many years? Is there patina or other natural build-up in the grooves of the carving? Etc.

Some Stones are Fakes

It is true that some of the Ica stones are fakes. Does this fact, however, force an honest investigator of the stones to reject the entire collection? No, it does not, for several reasons. First, if a stone is identified as a fake, there must be a way to prove it is fake. It must have fresh cut lines, no signs of patina, or no carved information that would be impossible for a person in modern times to obtain. If these same tests are applied to other stones, and those stones show signs of ancient wear, grooves that are not freshly hewn, and knowledge unavailable to modern carvers, then the authentic could be distinguished from the fake. Second, in other areas of life, it would not be acceptable to toss out legitimate articles based on the existence of fakes. If someone discovers a fake Rembrandt, should all Rembrandts be dismissed as frauds? Certainly not. Third, the fact that some stones are fakes could suggest that original, authentic stones exist as the models for the fakes. Fourth, if finding a forged stone would disprove the entire collection, what would stop a militant atheistic evolutionist from simply faking a stone or paying someone to do so? It certainly would not be surprising for those opposed to the biblical account to cast suspicion on the collection using fake stones. A classic rhetorical tactic is to build

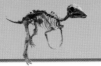

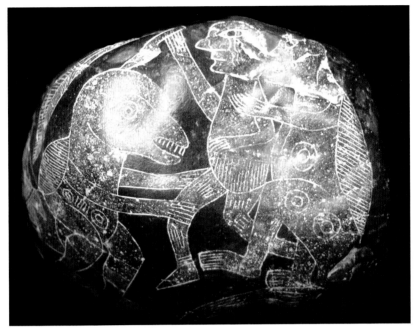

Bible.ca

a straw man that does not accurately represent the complete argument, tear it down, and then claim victory. Rejecting the entire collection, based on the fact that there are some faked stones, is nothing more than a straw man argument.

Fifth, the stories of alleged forgery fail to deal adequately with the prodigious number of stones that have been collected. Supposedly, a farmer named Basilio Uchuya and his wife Irma manufactured multiplied thousands of the stones and sold them to Dr. Cabrera. Yet, the site from which they allegedly quarried the stone is far too small to have yielded the massive amount of rock necessary for the collection, especially in light of the fact that many of the stones were large boulders that weighed several hundred pounds each. Along these lines,

Swift noted: "Such an enormous quantity of stones would have required an excavation on the scale of an open pit mine. It seems reasonable that they would have needed a vast array of modern equipment…. The sheer magnitude of such a mining operation would have left a huge crater. There is no way that such an operation could have escaped detection…" (n.d.[b], p. 24; see pp. 23-27 for more extensive material).

EVIDENCE OF THE STONES' AUTHENTICITY

Numerous reasons to accept the authenticity of the stones present themselves. Dennis Swift has listed several of these reasons in his book *Secrets of the Ica Stones and Nazca Lines.* Two extremely powerful arguments need to be considered.

First, Swift obtained a stone from a Nazca tomb that was excavated in 2001. The stone depicted a sauropod dinosaur. Swift also had Basilio Uchuya carve a fraudulent stone, both of which Swift submitted to intense microscopic analysis. The stone from the Nazca tomb contained human hair and scalp tissues and other evidence of age. Swift noted:

This stone had a heavy coat of patination and oxidation. Microorganisms could be seen in the grooves and the incisions. There is a uniformity of coloration and weathering. The incisions and cuts are as dark and weathered as the rest of the stone. There are several thick concentrations of salt peter that are so full of salt buildup that it covers parts of the carving with a white layer obscuring

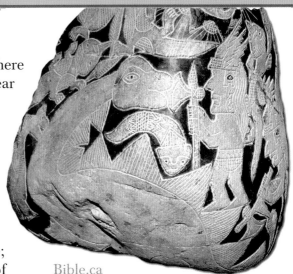

the image below.... There is notable irregular wear on the edges of the incisions that leads one to the inescapable conclusion that this stone had undergone considerable wear.... The salient conclusion of the laboratory is that the stone is of some age; in fact of antiquity of hundreds or thousands of years old (n.d.[b], p. 71).

Bible.ca

When submitted to microscopic analysis, the forged stone carved by Basilio was easily distinguished from the ancient stone as a modern creation. Tiny pieces of metal from the tool Basilio used were readily visible. The shallow scratches and chips were "clean and angled. There was no patina or film of oxidation on the stone; no microorganisms or salt peter were found on the stone. The laboratory conclusion was that the stone was of recent manufacture" (n.d.[b], p. 69). Just like a counterfeit dollar bill, the known forgery was easily distinguished from the authentic stone found in the tomb.

Second, the stones exhibit numerous depictions of dinosaurs, many of which are sauropods. Interestingly, the sauropods have dermal spines just like the Acambaro figurines. Allegedly, the stones were carved by modern forgers in the 1950s and 1960s, who gleaned their ideas of dinosaur anatomy from movies, comic books, and magazines. But dermal spines on sauropods were completely unknown at that time. It was not until Czerkas' discovery of fossilized skin impressions in 1992 that the modern world learned of the conical dermal spines that adorned the backs of sauropods. In the 1975 edition of his book *El Mensaje de las Piedras Grabadas de Ica* (*The Message of the Engraved Stones of Ica*), Dr. Javier Cabrera wrote extensively about the stones and included numerous photographs of them.

While many of Dr. Cabrera's ideas about aliens associated with the stones are quite bizarre, the concrete evidence portrayed in the pictures is not. Several pages contain pictures of sauropod dinosaurs that have the median row of dermal spines mentioned by Czerkas (1975, pp. 36-37, 65, 95, 97, 99,101). Many of the stones were found long before 1975, but the pictures are in a book published in that year, and thus must be at least 17 years prior to Czerkas' discovery. How would alleged forgers have known to put dermal spines on the sauropods? The most reasonable explanation is simply

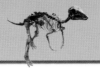
that there were no forgers. Ancient people saw the dinosaurs, interacted with them, and carved accurate pictures of them in stone hundreds of years ago.

CONCLUSION

If humans and dinosaurs lived together on the Earth in the past, what would you expect to find to verify their cohabitation? One line of conclusive evidence would be a series of carvings or drawings accurately depicting dinosaur anatomy that could be shown to have been produced before modern information about dinosaur anatomy emerged. The *Stegosaurus* carving in Cambodia, the dinosaur carving found by Samuel Hubbard, the accurate dinosaur petroglyph on Kachina Natural Bridge, dinosaur figurines discovered by Julsrud and studied by Charles Hapgood, the Ica stones, and various other carvings and figurines that we have not had space to include, converge to form a mountain of physical evidence that is exactly what would be expected if humans saw live dinosaurs. Evolutionists have used dinosaurs long enough to teach their false worldview. It is time to reclaim the dinosaurs, and use them to teach about the awesome power of the One Who created these magnificent creatures.

CHAPTER 6

Biblical Evidence for the Coexistence of Dinosaurs and Humans

Although evolutionists may be quick to discount anything that the Bible has to say about the coexistence of dinosaurs and humans, anyone who claims to be a Christian (and thus trusts the Bible to be God's revelation to man–2 Timothy 3:16-17; 2 Peter 1:20-21) should accept the information he or she finds in the Bible to be accurate. In regard to the coexistence of humans and dinosaurs, many modern-day "Bible believers" either have rejected what the Bible has to say on the subject, or else they never have given it much thought in light of various Bible passages. According to the Scriptures, the whole of God's earthly creation was brought

109

into existence in six days. Exodus 20:11 states: "For in six days the Lord made the heavens and the earth, the sea, and **all** that is in them, and rested the seventh day" (emp. added). This one verse should prove to the Christian that dinosaurs once lived together with humans.

Exodus 20:11 simply summarizes the Creation account of Genesis chapter 1 wherein the reader learns what was created on each day of Creation. In Genesis one, we find out that all animal life (whether sea creatures, land animals, or flying creatures) was created on days five and six of Creation—the sea creatures and flying animals on day five (Genesis 1:20-23) and land animals on day six (1:24-25). We also learn that God made the first humans, Adam and Eve, on day six (1:26-31). Thus, if all land animals were created on day six of Creation, and humans also were created on this day, then obviously humans and dinosaurs once lived as contemporaries. [NOTE: For evidence that the days of creation were literal, 24-hour days, see chapter 8.]

So why isn't the word "dinosaur" used in the Bible?

A college student once visited our offices and asked what he believed were troubling questions about the coexistence of dinosaurs and humans. One question that puzzled him was why dinosaurs are not mentioned in the Bible. "If God really did create dinosaurs, and if humans cohabited the Earth with them in the past, then surely we would read the word 'dinosaur' at least once in the Bible."

Admittedly, a person will not find the word "dinosaur" in most English translations of the Bible. However, this does not negate the fact that dinosaurs once cohabited the Earth with man. First, we must keep in mind that the Bible is not a taxonomical book. The Bible's main purpose is to tell us about God and His scheme of redemption, not to list every animal God created. The Bible mentions a **variety** of animals (including snakes, chickens, horses, goats, etc.), but not **every** animal. Simply because the Bible does not mention an animal does not mean that the Bible teaches the animal never existed alongside humans. There are many animals the Bible never specifically mentions, including kangaroos, elephants, aardvarks, anteaters, platypuses, and penguins. To say that these animals do not cohabit the Earth with man because the Bible does not mention them, would, of course, be false. To assume dinosaurs and humans never lived together on Earth because "the Bible doesn't mention dinosaurs," is equally erroneous.

Second, one must recognize that whereas the Bible was completed 1,900 years ago and was translated fully into English by 1535 (by Miles Coverdale), the English word

"dinosaur" was not coined until 1842–more than 300 years **after** the first complete English translation of the Old and New Testaments. Obviously, one would not expect to find the English term dinosaur–meaning "fearfully great" (*deinos*) "lizard" or "reptile" (*sauros*)–in a translation of the Bible that preceded its coinage.

Third, though most modern English Bible translators have elected to omit the term "dinosaur" in versions produced after 1842, such exclusion does not necessarily mean that Bible writers refrained from referring (either generally or specifically) to dinosaurs or dinosaur-like creatures. Consider the Hebrew term *tannin.* In Job 7:12, it is translated "sea monster" (ASV, NASB, RSV), "monster of the deep" (NIV), or "sea serpent" (NKJV). In Genesis 1:21 and Psalm 148:7 where the plural form of *tannin* is used (*tannim*) in literal contexts (like Job 7:12), the word is translated "great sea creatures/monsters" (NKJV, NIV, ASV, NASB, RSV). What are these "monsters" of the sea? No one knows for sure. It is possible that these are references to dinosaur-like, water-living reptiles (e.g., plesiosaurs). Also of interest is the fact that Isaiah referred to the "flying serpent" (30:6). Although it is impossible to know the exact identity of the "flying serpent,"

Drawing of a *Rhamphorynchus*

we do know that flying reptiles with long tails and slender bodies (e.g., *Rhamphorynchus, Dimorphodon*) once lived.

BEHEMOTH AND LEVIATHAN

In addition to the fact that the Bible clearly states that God made everything in six days (Genesis 1; Exodus 20:11), which by implication proves that dinosaurs once cohabited the Earth with man, God also described two creatures in the book of Job that sound very similar to dinosaurs or dinosaur-like, water-living reptiles. These creatures are known as behemoth and leviathan. Some deny the similarities between these animals and dinosaurs, suggesting that "attempts to link dinosaurs to 'behemoth' and 'leviathan' of Job do not stand up" (Clayton, 1996), while others doubt their actual existence altogether, believing them to be mythological creatures rather than literal animals. However, when a person unshackles himself from the chains of evolutionary thought (i.e., considering the possibility that dinosaurs and humans **did** live together at one time in the past and were not separated in time by 60+ million years), behemoth (of Job 40) and leviathan (of Job 41) are revealed neither as mythological nor modern-day, but extinct creatures that sound exactly like dinosaurs or (since the term "dinosaur" refers specifically to land-living reptiles) dinosaur-like, water-living reptiles.

MYTHOLOGICAL OR LITERAL?

For centuries, students of the Bible have questioned the identity of behemoth and leviathan. "In the Middle Ages, some theologians, like Albert Magnus, conceived of behemoth as a

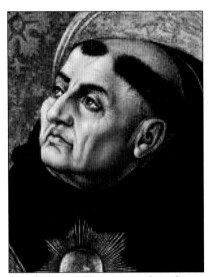

Depiction of Thomas Aquinas from the Demidoff Altarpiece

symbol of sensuality and sin. Others, like Thomas Aquinas, equated behemoth with the elephant, and leviathan with the whale" (Gordis, 1978, p. 569)–both being natural monsters in the **literal** sense, but representing diabolical power in a **figurative** sense. In 1663, Samuel Bochart published a two-volume work identifying the two animals under consideration as the hippopotamus and the crocodile. Then, as additional extrabiblical literature came to light in the middle-to-late nineteenth century (most notably from Mesopotamia), the mythological interpretation was revived and comparative mythology became very popular among biblical scholars.

By the closing of the nineteenth century, some scholars began to see mythology as the solution to the "identification problem" of the creatures described in Job 40-41. That problem was stated by T.K. Cheyne as early as 1887 when he observed that "neither Behemoth nor Leviathan corresponds strictly to any known animal" (p. 56). In 1892, C.H. Toy argued that behemoth and leviathan were water animals associated with the "primeval seas Apsu and Tiamat as they appeared to be presented in the emerging Babylonian Epic of Creation" (as quoted in Wilson, 1975, 25:2). Marvin Pope

probably is the most recent well-known supporter of the mythological view. Using the Ugaritic texts as support for his theory, Pope has proposed that behemoth and leviathan of Job 40-41 are the same mythological creatures found in the ancient Jewish writings of Enoch, IV Ezra, and the Apocalypse of Baruch (1965).

One reason why various scholars have held to the mythological view is simply because they believe that behemoth and leviathan cannot be the hippopotamus and the crocodile. It is obvious that the animals in Job 40-41 are represented as being beyond the power of men to capture. Yet it is known that ancient Egyptians hunted and captured both the crocodile and the hippopotamus (Driver and Gray, 1964, p. 353). Also, if the animals really are the hip-popotamus and the crocodile, one wonders why there is a shift from the Palestinian animals of the previous chapters to Egyptian animals in chapters 40-41. Mythologizers suggest that the animals described in

Job 40-41 are neither crocodiles, hippopotami, nor any other known creature. Thus, they conclude the animals described in these two chapters must be imaginary monsters.

What evidence is there to suggest that behemoth and leviathan of Job 40-41 are, in fact, real, literal animals, and not imaginary, mythological creatures? First, certain Old Testament passages clearly speak of leviathan and behemoth in various contexts without any hint whatsoever of mythological or symbolic import. Even though leviathan may refer to a mythological creature in Job 3:8 and Psalm 74:14, there is at least one passage (other than Job 41) that speaks of it as a real animal. In expressing his thoughts that the great sea monsters were created by Jehovah, the Psalmist wrote: "There the ships sail about; there is that leviathan which You have made to play there" (104:26). Furthermore, every time behemoth is mentioned outside of Job 40, it refers to real animals (Cansdale, 1996, p. 43). In differentiating between whether the passage is speaking of an imaginary or a literal creature, one must be guided by the thrust of the context, not by what similarities might be

Leviathan as depicted by Gustave Doré

found between pagan mythology and the Bible (Smick, 1978, 40[2]:214). In the context of Job 38-41, God is in the midst of asking Job a lengthy series of questions–the entire purpose of which was to show the patriarch that he did not know nearly as much as he thought he did when he charged God foolishly. If the creatures in Job 40-41 were, in fact, mythological, Job then could have turned to God and asked, "What is your point? These creatures are mythological." God's argument would have collapsed of its own weight. The context (which

also refers to other real animals such as horses, hawks, and ostriches) becomes critical, especially considering the purpose and intent of God's questions to Job. That leviathan was referred to in ancient mythological literature is beyond question. But this does not prove that mythological creatures are under consideration in Job 40 and 41.

Second, neither description is close to being identical with that of such monsters as depicted in any ancient Near Eastern mythology (see Wharton, 1999, p. 175). No mythical creature called behemoth, nor anything like it, is seen in pagan mythology (despite Marvin Pope's attempt to identify behemoth with "the ferocious bullock of El"). And, one of leviathan's most impressive characteristics—the ability to breathe fire—is not even mentioned in the ancient Ugaritic texts. It also is interesting to note that in Job 41, God does not mention leviathan having multiple heads, as is stated in the mythopoetic language of Psalm 74:14: "You broke the heads of leviathan in pieces." Mythology speaks of leviathan as having seven heads, but in the description of Job 41 we read that he has only one head (vs. 7), one tongue (vs. 1), one nose (vs. 2), and one jaw (vs. 2). There is absolutely no hint of Job's leviathan having multiple heads. Surely, if leviathan of Job 41 were a mythological creature, God would not have excluded such vital characteristics as these.

Third, instead of attempting to **prove** that these are mythological creatures, some mythologizers try to reason in a somewhat reverse fashion. They argue that since these creatures cannot be the hippopotamus and the crocodile, then

"Behemoth" by Lewis Lavoie

they must be mythological (Driver and Gray, 1964, p. 351). This kind of logic is faulty, however, as it closes its parameters to another very real possibility–extinct creatures.

118

Fourth, although the poems in Job 40-41 are longer and are placed into the context of a separate speech, essentially they are the same as the earlier poems which deal with familiar birds and animals that the reader would have been expected to know (Anderson, 1974, p. 289). From the existence of these animals, God obviously intended Job to draw important conclusions regarding the nature of the world and man's place in it. Robert Gordis commented: "The same consideration supports the idea that Behemoth and Leviathan are also natural creatures, the existence of which heightens the impact of God's argument" (1978, p. 571). Descriptions of these creatures are critical in regard to the intent of God's speeches to Job. "They are surely to be taken...as variations on the theme that God is God and Job is not" (Wharton, p. 174). Job is overwhelmed by the "sheer power and terror of these beings, but even more so by the fact that they exist as signs of God's overarching power" (Wharton, p. 174). In contemplating taking up his case with God, Job has been concerned with being overcome by terror (cf. 9:32-35; 13:20-21). Now Jehovah is showing Job that his apprehensions were not misplaced. If he would have to retreat in terror before a literal animal like leviathan, he certainly was unfit to contend in court with Almighty God!

Fifth, allowing for the use of highly poetic language at times, the book of Job remains realistic throughout (Anderson, 1974, p. 288). Job was a **real** person (cf. Ezekiel 14:14,20; James 5:11) who experienced **real** pain. He challenged a **real** God that was (and is) alive. Jehovah described **real** creatures in Job

38 and 39. And so there is no legitimate reason for rejecting behemoth and leviathan as **real animals**.

Sixth, unlike the mythology in the Babylonian and Ugaritic creation epics (where the writers described alleged cosmic events of the distant **past**), God was concerned in His discussion with Job with the appearance and habits of these creatures in the **present**. God "is not interested in imaginary creatures from the dim mythological past—he is concerned with the actual present, with the vast universe as it is governed by its Maker" (Gordis, 1965, p. 119).

Finally, that these creatures are real would seem to be quite conclusive, for Job 40:15 states explicitly that behemoth and Job are equally God's creatures (Anderson, 1974, pp. 288-289). Speaking to Job, God said, "Behold now, **behemoth, which I made** as well as thee" (40:15, emp. added).

Those who take the mythological approach when interpreting Job 40-41 simply are making comparisons to their liking. They have been so captivated by "apparent" parallels in ancient literature that they have lost sight of the basic exegetical test—the relevance and appropriateness of the interpretation within the context of the book of Job (Gordis, 1978, p. 569).

IDENTIFYING BEHEMOTH AND LEVIATHAN

So what are these flesh-and-blood creatures that God employed to impress upon Job his puniness when compared with God's omnipotence? Older expositors like Thomas Aquinas thought that perhaps

behemoth was the elephant, while leviathan was the whale (e.g., Gibson, 1905, p. 220). But since Samuel Bochart's two-volume work *Hierozoicon, sive bipertitum opus de animalibus Sacrae Scripturae* was published in 1663, most modern critics have labeled the animals in question as the hippopotamus and the crocodile (Wilson, 1975, 25:1). Their basic claim is that the hippopotamus fits many of the characteristics of behemoth, while the crocodile aligns itself very closely with leviathan. This position has become so popular in modern times that few commentators have bothered to challenge the proposed identification of these beasts. In fact, even some versions of the Bible identify these creatures in the marginal notes or chapter headings as the hippopotamus and the crocodile.

When commenting on behemoth and leviathan, modern scholars who do not hold to the mythological view often choose to make a general statement like, "Most identify these beasts as the hippo and the crocodile." But then they give little if any evidence to support such a claim. Another disturbing trend is how "certain" many of the commentators sound when identifying these animals. For example, Gordis confidently stated: "Behemoth is to be identified as the hippopotamus and Leviathan

as the crocodile" (1978, p. 571). Edgar Gibson wrote: "There can be little doubt that" behemoth corresponds with the hippopotamus, and "there can be no doubt here leviathan means the crocodile" (1905, p. 223). In his practical book on Job, Theodore Epp confidently affirmed: "The first animal mentioned is the behemoth or the hippopotamus" and the leviathan "was a large crocodile" (1967, p. 175). Again, however, after making such definite statements, little evidence is offered, except for making a few comparisons between the animals. Actually, in more than one commentary, the reader will find ample time spent answering objections, but little to none laying out concrete evidence supporting the author's particular theory.

The Hippopotamus and the Crocodile?

While it is true that a few similarities do exist between behemoth and the hippo and the leviathan and the crocodile, many of the descriptive details do not seem to fit either creature. These differences are so numerous and significant that they cannot be overlooked.

1. It has been suggested by some scholars that the word behemoth itself derives from a hypothetical Egyptian compound *p'-ih-mw* (*pehemu*), meaning "the ox of the water" (Mitchell, 1996, p. 127). But, as Marvin Pope observed, "no such word has yet been found in

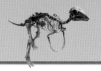

Coptic or Egyptian and no known Egyptian designation of the hippopotamus bears any close resemblance to the word Behemoth" (1965, p. 268).

2. God described behemoth as a creature that "moves his tail like a cedar" (40:17). The tail of a hippopotamus "would surely not have been compared to a cedar by a truthful though poetic observer like the author of chapters 38-39" (Cheyne, 1887, p. 56). The hippopotamus hardly could be described—with its little 6-8 inch stubby appendage—as having a stiff or large tail. The tail of the hippo is short and small like that of a pig, and is a mere twig in comparison with a cedar tree. But that fact has not prevented commentators from attempting to avoid the obvious. Edgar Gibson wrote: "The comparison of the short, stiff, muscular tail, to the strong and elastic cedar branch (which is probably intended) seems really to be perfectly natural, and need cause no difficulty" (1905, p. 221, parenthetical comment in orig.). Keil and Delitzsch also concluded that the tail should not be compared to the cedar **tree**, but the cedar **branch** (1996). Hartley has advocated the view

Cedar Tree

123

that the tail (*zanab*) is being compared to a cedar tree, rather than to a branch, but that God really was referring to the genitals of the hippopotamus (1988, p. 525). However, there is no credible evidence that *zanab* was used euphemistically in Hebrew (e.g., as in regard to the genitals), while referring only to analogies in English or other languages (Pope, 1965, p. 324). It appears that Hartley and others have rejected the logical rendering of the passage in order to force a comparison between behemoth and the hippopotamus.

3. Behemoth is said to be "**chief** of the ways of God" (40:19, ASV, emp. added). What does it mean to be "chief" or "first of the ways of God" (NKJV)? After analyzing the Hebrew word for "chief/first" (*re'sit*–pronounced ray-shees) as well as the context in which it is found, Dave Miller wrote:

We are forced to conclude that when God referred to behemoth as the "first" or "chief" of His ways, He was referring primarily, if not exclusively, to its **size and strength**. God was challenging Job with his inability to tame, subdue, or control this massive creature (even as the next animal with which God confronts Job, leviathan, is noted for its ferocity [Job 41]). Of the other 50 occurrences of *re'sit*, Jeremiah 49:35 comes closest to the sense intended in Job 40:19. Various translations render the term "**mainstay** of their might" (NIV), "**foremost** of their might" (NKJV), "**chief** of their might" (KJV, ASV), and "**finest** of their might" (NASB)—all referring to strength, power, and force.

This conclusion is supported contextually in Job by the fact that the line of reasoning God uses in chapters 38-41 is that Job is incapable of understanding, controlling, directing, or regulating the various aspects of the created order that God placed before him—from the 19 inanimate wonders of the Universe and Earth in 38:1-38, to the nine animals in 38:39-39:30, building to the grand and climactic final two creatures, behemoth and leviathan, in 40:15-41:34....

This conclusion is further supported by behemoth's specific features that God brings to Job's attention—features that inherently imply size, mass, weight, bulk, and strength: "his **strength** is in his **hips**" (vs. 16), "his **power** is in his **stomach muscles**" (vs. 16), "he moves his tail **like a cedar**" (vs. 17), "his bones are like **beams of bronze**" (vs. 18), "his ribs like **bars of iron**" (vs. 18). The context lends further support to "first" referring to size, due to the parallel clause that follows...: "**Only He who made him can bring near His sword**."

...The point of this passage is obvious: the gargantuan behemoth is of such stature and strength that only the

Creator can control it. He is "the chief of the ways of God" (2008).

Surely this would rule out the hippo, since at full size it is but seven feet high (Thompson and Bromling, n.d., p. 5). An elephant is twice the size of a hippopotamus, and yet even it was dwarfed by certain dinosaurs. The dinosaur once popularly referred to as *Brontosaurus* (now known more accurately as *Apatosaurus*) grew to weigh more than 30 tons, whereas the hippo weighs in at only around four tons (Jackson, 1983, p. 86). What's more, scientists estimate that *Argentinosaurus* reached lengths of 120 feet and weights of over 100 tons. From everything currently known about animals of the past and present—no land animal came close to reaching the same size as the largest dinosaurs. They were "chief of the ways of God."

"The Hippopotamus Hunt"
Peter Paul Ruben
1617

4. The text indicates that no man could approach behemoth with a sword (40:19), nor was he able to capture him (40:24). Yet as mentioned earlier, the hippopotamus was hunted frequently and captured successfully by the Egyptians (Driver and Gray, 1964, p. 353). Hartley observed:

> Egyptian pharaohs took pride in slaying a hippopotamus. There are numerous pictures in which the pharaoh, hunting a hippopotamus from a papyrus boat, is poised to hurl his harpoon into the animal's opened mouth, thereby inflicting a fatal blow (1988, p. 524).

Egyptians even celebrated festivals known as "Harpooning the Hippopotamus" (Hartley, 1988, p. 524). Additionally, Egyptian monuments frequently picture single hunters attacking the hippo with a spear (McClintock and Strong, 1968, 1:728). How could one accurately compare the unapproachable and unseizable behemoth with the hippopotamus?

HUNTING IN THE MARSHES: ENCOUNTERING AND SPEARING A HIPPOPOTAMUS.[1]
[1] Tomb of Ti. Drawn by Faucher-Gudin, from DÜMICHEN, *Resultate*, vol. ii. pl. x.

5. Leviathan also is represented as unapproachable and too mighty to be apprehended by men. The Lord said:

> Can you draw out leviathan with a hook, or snare his tongue with a line which you lower? Can you put a reed through his nose, or pierce his jaw with a hook?... Though the sword reaches him, it cannot avail; nor does spear, dart, or javelin (41:1-2,26).

It is clear that the leviathan is represented as "too powerful and ferocious for mere man to dare to come to grips with it" (Pope, p. 268). He is "beyond the power of men to capture" (Driver and Gray, 1964, p. 353). Leviathan is "peerless and fearless" (Strauss, 1976, p. 437). Contrariwise, the crocodile—like the hippopotamus—was hunted and captured by Egyptians. Herodotus discussed how they captured crocodiles (Rowley, 1980, p. 259), and how that, after being seized, some even were tamed (Jackson, 1983, p. 87). Other crocodiles were mummified (see Hoffman, 2002, 87[16]:10-12). Such a scene hardly depicts the animal of Job 40:15ff.

6. God also described leviathan as an animal that cannot be availed by swords, spears, or darts (41:26). In fact, leviathan "laughs at the threat of javelins" (41:29) and "his undersides are like sharp potsherds" (41:30). In commenting on these verses, Thompson and Bromling wrote:

> Although the hide that covers the crocodile's back is extremely thick and difficult to penetrate, this is not true of his belly. The crocodile is most vulnerable to spears and javelins on his underside; hence, it could not be said of him that "his underparts are like sharp potsherds" (n.d., p. 7).

7. According to God, leviathan's "sneezings flash forth light, and his eyes are like the eyelids of the morning. Out of his mouth go burning lights; sparks of fire shoot out. Smoke goes out of his nostrils, as from a boiling pot and burning rushes. His breath kindles coals, and a flame goes out of his mouth" (Job 41:18-21). Although some have scoffed at this description of leviathan (assuming that no animal ever has had such "fire-breathing" abilities), it is not impossible physiologically, as various scientists have pointed out (see for example DeYoung, 2000, pp. 117-118; Morris, 1984, p. 359). What should be evident to everyone, however, is that this unique description sounds nothing like a crocodile. [NOTE: For a discussion on fire-breathing dragons, see chapters 2 and 3.]

The problem of identifying these two creatures was acknowledged by T.K. Cheyne long ago. Even though his mythological interpretation of Job 40-41 is faulty, he and others have observed correctly that neither

behemoth nor leviathan corresponds well to the hippopotamus or the crocodile. If Edwin Good was speaking of present-day animals, he was correct when he wrote: "There is simply no plausible natural counterpart to Leviathan" (1990, p. 361). Plus, "[e]ating grass like the cattle, having a tail in any way comparable to a cedar, having any contact with the mountains, and relating to the Jordan River, are all incompatibilities between Behemoth and the hippopotamus" (Wolfers, 1995, p. 191). Actually, the only support for identification of behemoth as the hippopotamus is the biblical description "not of the animal but of its habitat" (Good, 1990, p. 358).

Concerning leviathan, Wolfers wrote: "Underside like sharpest potsherds, swimming in sea rather than river, and breathing fire and smoke, are incompatibilities between Leviathan and the crocodile" (p. 191). Job 41 is dominated by the idea of the beast's utter invincibility. As Driver and Gray admitted: "There is nothing, unless we should so regard 41:7, that points necessarily or at all striking to the crocodile, and one or two points seem inconsistent with it" (1964, p. 353). In reality, there are more than just "one or two points" that are inconsistent with the suggestion that the leviathan is little more than a crocodile.

Behemoth as a Dinosaur; Leviathan as a Water-Living Reptile?

The evidence documents overwhelmingly that behemoth and leviathan of Job 40-41 were flesh-and-blood animals, not imaginary creatures. Furthermore, the description of these creatures does not fit that of any known animal present in the

world today, regardless of attempts to equate them with the hippopotamus and the crocodile. Thus, they must be some type of extinct creature. But what kind? God's descriptions of behemoth and leviathan are compatible in every way with the descriptions we have of dinosaurs and dinosaur-like, water-living reptiles that roamed the Earth, not millions of years ago as some have suggested, but only a few thousand years ago. Moses wrote: "For in six days Jehovah made heaven and earth, the sea, and **all** that in them is" (Exodus 20:11, emp. added). Man, according to Christ, existed "from the beginning of the creation" (Mark 10:6; cf. Matthew 19:4). So did the dinosaurs. Bible believers must admit the possibility that behemoth and leviathan could have been dinosaurs.

Well-known progressive creationist Hugh Ross ridiculed the concept that the biblical creatures, behemoth and leviathan, were dinosaurs or dinosaur-like animals. According to Ross, "No dinosaur...ever breathed fire or smoke or had bones of iron and brass" (1998, p. 48). Ross has chosen to believe that the magnificent creatures described by God in His second speech to Job were the hippopotamus and the crocodile. [NOTE: For a response to Ross's allegations that "No dinosaur...ever breathed fire or smoke," see chapter 3.]

Like so many professed Christians who have tried to amalgamate the long evolutionary ages with the biblical

131

account of Creation, Ross's reservations to accept the likelihood of behemoth being a dinosaur and leviathan being a dinosaur-like, water-living reptile are not the result of a sensible, judicious exegesis of the biblical text. A man who believes that dinosaurs "dominated the Earth's land and sea life from 250 million to 65 million years ago" (p. 48), and that "no credible evidence whatever suggests the coexistence of primates and the great dinosaurs" (p. 49), obviously will have a difficult time accepting that behemoth and leviathan (which existed at the same time as Job) were dinosaurs or dinosaur-like animals.

One of the main reasons Ross gives for rejecting the dinosaur-like features of these creatures is that "no creatures on Earth, alive or extinct, fit the literal descriptions." Yet, we wonder if Ross could answer a question for us: Although admittedly no creature **alive today** fits the "literal descriptions" of leviathan and behemoth, how can Ross confidently assert that **no extinct animal** resembles the description of behemoth or leviathan? How does Ross know the description of every creature that has lived on the Earth? How does he know what feats they were capable of performing? Ross might suggest: "But common sense tells us that no creature had ribs of 'iron' or bones of 'brass' " (cf. Job 40:18). True. But when God employed such metaphors and similes, any reasonable Bible student can understand that He was stressing the fact that behemoth's bones were incredibly solid—**like** they were made of solid metal. Interestingly, although dinosaurs had the largest, most massive bones of any known animal that

"Leviathan" by Lewis Lavoie

has ever walked the Earth (e.g., one fossilized *Argentinosaurus* vertebra was five feet high and five feet wide—see Meyer, 2002), and even though they are known to have the most massive tails of any animal ever known (e.g., the 40-foot-long tail of *Diplodocus*), which could reasonably be likened to a "cedar" (Job 40:17), Ross has chosen rather to believe that behemoth was a hippo—an animal with a tail shorter than many dogs and cats.

The fact is, three possible explanations exist for the exact identity of the biblical creatures known as behemoth and leviathan (of Job 40-41): (1) they are unreal, mythological monsters; (2) they are real animals that exist somewhere in

133

the world today; or (3) they are some kind of real, yet extinct creature. The biblical and scientific evidence makes it clear that the third choice is the logical option. Yet, sadly, as Henry Morris has observed:

> Modern Bible scholars, for the most part, have become so conditioned to think in terms of the long ages of evolutionary geology that it never occurs to them that mankind once lived in the same world with the great animals that are now found only as fossils (1988, p. 115).

[NOTE: For a discussion on the incompatibility of the Bible's timeline with the evolutionary billion-year timeline, see chapter 8.]

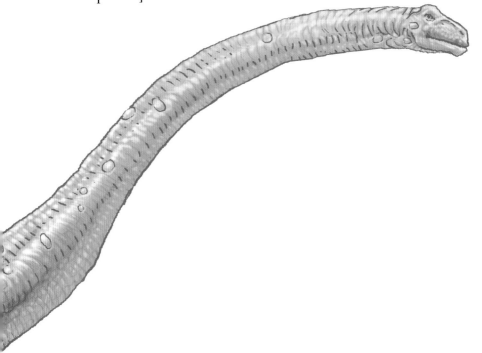

CHAPTER 7

Fossils, Dinosaurs, and Humans

WHERE IS THE FOSSIL EVIDENCE FOR THE COEXISTENCE OF DINOSAURS AND HUMANS?

If dinosaurs and humans really did live as contemporaries on Earth at one time, why is it that human fossils have not been found alongside, near, or in the same strata as dinosaur fossils? If they lived together and died together, shouldn't there be evidence from the fossil record of their coexistence?

Admittedly, sometimes questions like these appear rather puzzling. We know from Scripture that dinosaurs and humans coexisted (cf. Exodus 20:11). Furthermore, various ancient paintings, figurines, rock carvings, and historical references confirm they were contemporaries upon the Earth. (How could humans have drawn and described dinosaurs so accurately if they never saw dinosaurs?) Still, many wonder why, at first glance, the fossil record seems not to substantiate creationists' claims that dinosaurs and humans were contemporaries.

FOSSILIZATION IS RARE

First, one must understand that fossils are rare, relatively speaking. Not every living plant, animal, or human fossilizes after death. In fact, it is **extremely rare** for things once living to fossilize. Dead animals lying in a field or on the side of the road do not fossilize. In order for something to become fossilized, it must be buried rapidly in just the right place. Consider, as an example, all the bison that were killed and left to decompose on the Great Plains of the United States. In the late 19th century, a man could purchase a window seat on a train, have the conductor stop close to a herd of American bison, and pull out his rifle and fire upon the herd until he ran out of ammunition. The locomotive would then move on, leaving behind countless dead and dying animals. By the end of the 19th century, the bison population in America had been reduced from millions to approximately 500 (Jones, n.d.). What happened to the millions of carcasses? They are not scattered all along

the Great Plains today. Why? Because their flesh and bones were scavenged by insects, worms, birds, and other animals. The smallest portions were digested by fungi, bacteria, and enzymatic degradation until the buffalo remains disappeared. Even oxygen plays a role in the breakdown of chemicals that make up living things.

Evolutionary scientist James Powell described another situation where a rather large population of animals died. He wrote:

> [I]n the winter after the great Yellowstone fires of 1988, thousands of elk perished from extreme cold coupled with lack of food. Late the following spring, their carcasses were strewn everywhere. Yet only a few years later, bones from the great elk kill are scarce. The odds that a single one will be preserved so that it can be found 65 million years from now approach zero. At best we can expect to find fossil evidence of only a **tiny fraction** of the animals that once lived. The earth's normal processes destroy or hide most of the clues (1998, p. xv, emp. added).

Normally, as Powell indicated, living things do not fossilize. Under **normal** conditions, living things decay and rot. It is **atypical** for plants and animals to fossilize, because they must avoid even the tiniest of scavengers, bacteria, fungi, etc. For bones to fossilize, they must be buried—the sooner and deeper, the better. Mud, silt, and other fine sediments are good for fossilization because they can block out oxygen. In this "protected" environment, bones and teeth may even last long enough to mineralize. But, **normally**, carcasses do not find themselves in such environments.

NOT AS MANY DINOSAUR FOSSILS AS YOU THINK

Although dinosaur graveyards have been discovered in various countries around the world (e.g., Tanzania, Africa; Jenson, Utah [USA]) where thousands of dinosaur bones are jumbled together (obviously due to some sort of catastrophe—e.g., a flood), most people are unaware of the fact that, in museums, "in spite of the intense popular and scientific interest in the dinosaurs and the well-publicized efforts of generations of dinosaur hunters, only about 2,100 articulated dinosaur bones (two or more aligned in the same position as in life)" exist (Powell, 1998, p. xv, parenthetical item in orig.; see also Dodson, 1990, 87:7608; Lewin, 1990, 128[1745]). Furthermore, in an article in the October 1990 issue of the *Proceedings of the National Academy of Sciences*, Peter Dodson of the University of Pennsylvania reported that almost half (45.3%) of all dinosaur genera are based on a **single** specimen, and 74% are represented by five specimens or less (87:7608). Even

some of the most famous dinosaurs are based on a fraction of what they were originally. For example, the 120-foot-long *Argentinosaurus* replica (housed in the Fernbank Museum of Natural History in Atlanta, Georgia) is based on only 10 percent of its remains (a dozen backbone vertebrae, a few limb bones and part of the hips) [Meyer, 2002]. Truthfully, although dinosaurs have captured the attention of scientists for more than 150 years, their fossilized remains are not as prevalent as many would think.

Human Fossils—Extremely Scarce!

Humans make up an infinitesimal portion of the fossil record. Due to the number of drawings of our alleged human ancestors that appear in the news on a regular basis, one might get the feeling that hominoid and human fossils are ubiquitous. But such is not the case. In a 1981 *New Scientist* article, John Reader wrote: "The entire hominid collection known today would barely cover a billiard table" (89:802).

One year later, Lyall Watson similarly stated: "The fossils that decorate our family tree are so scarce that there are still more scientists than specimens. The remarkable fact is that **all the physical evidence we have for human evolution can still be placed, with room to spare, inside a single coffin**" (1982, 90[5]:44, emp. added). It is true, of course, that additional alleged hominid fossils have been discovered since Watson and Reader made their comments, but none qualifies as a legitimate human ancestor (see Harrub and Thompson, 2003, pp. 14ff.). In a conversation with James Powell, president and director of the Los Angeles County Museum of Natural History, renowned evolutionary paleoanthropologist Meave Leakey gave some insight into her frustrations in searching for hominid (or human) fossils when she described her "nearly futile hunt for human bone in a new field area as **four years** of hard work producing only **three nondescript scraps**" (see Powell, 1998, p. xv, emp. added). More recently, David Begun concluded an article in *Science* titled, "The Earliest Hominins—Is Less More?," by admitting: "[T]he level of uncertainty in the available direct evidence at this time renders irreconcilable differences of opinion inevitable. The solution is in the mantra of all paleontologists: **We need more fossils!**" (2004, 303:1479-1480, emp. added). Although hominid/human fossils are among the most sought-after fossils in the world, scientists readily admit that few such fossils have been found.

As you can see, the question "Why don't we find dinosaur and human fossils together?" is extremely misleading. The truth is, fossils themselves are rare. And, of all those things that

do fossilize, it appears that less than 1% are vertebrates (fish, amphibians, reptiles, birds, or mammals) [see Snelling, 1991, 14[1]:30]. Furthermore, **human fossils** make up a microscopic part of the fossil record. Searching for one is like trying to find the one proverbial needle in a haystack. The real question then, is not, "Why don't we find dinosaur and human fossils together?," but, "Where are all of the human fossils?"

Dodo bird

Simply because human fossils apparently have not been found with dinosaur fossils does not make the case for the coexistence of dinosaurs and humans any less credible. Think about it. Where are the human fossils that have been found with the recently extinct Pyrenean Ibex? Can we prove that Dodo birds and humans once lived together by observing their fossilized remains together in a particular layer of rock? We know that they once coexisted, but can a person point to the fossil record for such information? The chance of finding human fossils is rare. The chance of finding exactly the combination of fossils for which one is searching (in this case, dinosaurs and humans) is even less likely.

A LESSON LEARNED FROM "LIVING FOSSILS"

We learn from "living fossils" that animals and plants can live long periods of time (allegedly millions of years) **without leaving behind fossil evidence**. For example, evolutionists believe Gingko trees were thriving 240 million years ago, **before** dinosaurs allegedly evolved (see Krock, 2003). Interestingly, Gingko fossils are absent in rock layers reportedly representing many millions of years, yet they are alive today (Hodge, 2006, p. 183). Consequently, simply because they are absent in certain rock strata does not mean they were non-existent during the alleged millions of years it took those layers of rock to form. Likewise, simply because human fossils are missing in certain layers of rock does not mean they were not living at the time those rock layers were formed.

Consider also the living fossil known as the coelacanth. From 1839 (when fossil coelacanths were first discovered–Perkins, 2001) to 1938, evolutionists alleged that these fish were the missing link in the evolution of fish to amphibians ("Diver Finds...,"

Ginko tree and leaves

Republic of South Africa stamp showing coelacanth

n.d.). Supposedly, coelacanths had existed "for nearly 400 million years" ("Diver Finds…"). Evolutionists firmly believed that "the coelacanth became extinct about 70 million years ago [about the same time dinosaurs died out– EL/KB] because their fossils are not found in any deposits higher than this" (Hodge, 2006, p. 183). *Science News* declared that coelacanths **"disappeared from the fossil record 75 million years ago"** (Perkins, 2001, emp. added). Until 1938, evolutionists believed that men and coelacanths could not possibly have lived at the same time. These creatures were known only from rock layers that evolutionists claimed were 70+ million years old.

On December 24, 1938, the scientific world was rocked when an unidentified fish five feet long and over 100 pounds was brought to shore in South Africa. It was caught in the Indian Ocean near Madagascar. The fisherman who netted the fish (having no idea what the creature's proper name was) called it "the great sea lizard" because its pectoral fins looked more like little fringed legs. Once scientists examined this strange creature, however, they confirmed what formerly was thought impossible– a live coelacanth had been caught in modern times (see "Coelacanth," n.d.)!

143

It was as shocking as if a living *T. rex* had been found. After all, they supposedly became extinct at the same time.

Since 1938, more than 100 coelacanths have been caught and many more sighted (see "Coelacanth"). In 1952, they were seen swimming near the Comoro Islands in the Indian Ocean. Another population was found in 1998 off the coast of Indonesia. Surprisingly, local Indonesian fishermen were quite familiar with this fish, having been catching them for years: Yet scientists were totally unaware they lived in that region.

Modern-day coelacanths look exactly like their fossil counterparts (which are **mistakenly** dated as being millions of years old). This "living fossil" is a thorn in the side of evolutionists. It makes a mockery of evolutionary dating methods, provides further proof of the myths of missing links, and exposes their "facts" for what they really are—unproven assumptions.

Moreover, consider that evolutionists admit that the fossil record of the past "70 million years" shows no evidence of coelacanths. Yet, we know they lived during these alleged "70 million years," because they are still alive today. Like Gingko trees, coelacanths' absence in certain rock strata does not mean they were not living during the alleged millions of years it took the rock layers to form; it simply means that they were not buried and fossilized in those layers of rock.

144

Similarly, humans just as easily could have been alive when the various rock layers were formed, without leaving human fossils. Think about it: we have just as much fossil evidence for humans living the past "70 million years" on Earth as we do coelacanths and Gingkos. In short, living fossils help us understand that simply because human fossils are missing in certain layers of rock does not mean humans were not living at the time those rock layers were formed.

SLIM CHANCE

Considering that sedimentary rock (the type of rock in which fossils are most likely to be discovered) covers about 75% of earth's land area and much of the ocean floor, and is

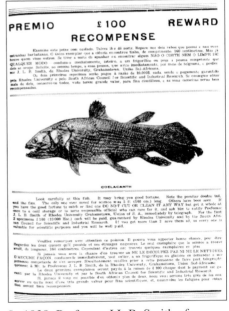

In 1939, Professor J.L.B. Smith of Rhodes University in England offered a reward to those who could catch a coelacanth.

145

tens of thousands of feet thick in certain places (Crawford, 1988, 17:278), even if there are dinosaur and human remains fossilized in the same rock, the chance of them being exposed, discovered, recognized, and reported together is very improbable. They might be exposed somewhere in the world today (like a mine, cliff, or road cutting), but unless they are discovered before the Sun, wind, and rain turn them to dust, such exposure is useless to scientists.

HUMANS AND THE FLOOD

It could be that in the time of Noah, the human population was confined mainly to the Middle East, while most dinosaurs roamed in other parts of the world. If this was the case, and the global Flood of Noah's day caused most of the fossils on Earth (as creationists believe), then one would not expect to find many (if any) humans buried with dinosaurs. What's more, humans would have been less likely (than various animals) to be buried rapidly and fossilized during the Flood. As Bodie Hodge noted:

> Since the rains of Noah's Flood took weeks to cover the earth, many people could have made it to boats, grabbed on to floating debris, and so on. Some may have made it to higher ground. Although they wouldn't have lasted long and would have eventually perished, they might not fossilize (Hodge, 2006, p. 179).

The fact is, in most cases, living things do not fossilize.

> [D]ead things decompose or get eaten. They just disappear and nothing is left. The 2004 tsunami in Southeast Asia was a shocking reminder of the speed

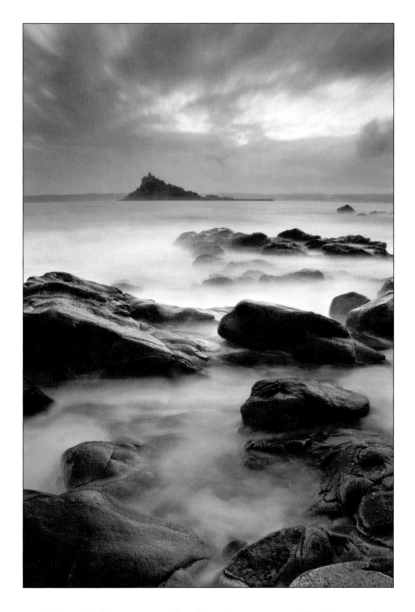

with which water and other forces can eliminate all trace of bodies, even when we know where to look. According to the United Nation's Office of the Special Envoy for Tsunami Recovery, nearly 43,000 tsunami victims were never found (Hodge, p. 180).

COULD IT BE...?

It may very well be the case that human and dinosaur bones **have been discovered together** in times past, but for at least two reasons, were not reported. First, someone who might have found these bones in a quarry could react by saying, "Look at these old bones. Fascinating!... Okay, now, hurry up and hand me another explosive so we can meet our quota of coal for the day." It could be that the fossil evidence for the cohabitation of men and dinosaurs went up in smoke long ago. Second, it may be possible that human bones **have** been found by scientists alongside dinosaur fossils, yet simply have not been reported widely. We are not suggesting that all evolutionary scientists are dishonest. Rather, we simply believe they are blinded by presuppositions that affect their judgment. Since evolutionists seem so certain that hominid/human fossils should never be found in layers of rock more than a few million years old, if they ever did, likely they would just explain away the evidence. "It just cannot be, if evolution is true.... There must be some explanation other than that humans and dinosaurs really lived

together." If evolutionists can "confuse" a dolphin's rib for a human collarbone (Anderson, 1983, p. 199), or an extinct pig's tooth for a human tooth (e.g., Nebraska Man; see Harrub and Thompson, 2003, pp. 88-89), then similar mistakes could easily be made concerning human and dinosaur fossils. If one ever has been found with the other, scientists could have misinterpreted the "anomaly."

MAMMALS AND THE FOSSIL RECORD

Conventional evolutionary theory not only says that humans and dinosaur never lived together, but that the only mammals which had evolved during the time of the dinosaurs were "small, mostly about mouse-sized, and rare" (Simpson, et al., 1957). "[E]arly mammals were timid, chipmunk-sized creatures that scurried in the looming shadow of the giant reptiles" (Verrengia, 2005). In 2002, on the cover of *U.S. News and World Report* were the words "The New Reality of Evolution." After the overly confident cover-story author, Thomas Hayden, assured everyone that evolution is a "fundamental fact" (2002, 133[4]:43), he then paraded various alleged facts before the reader, including the following:

> We may owe our own dominance to the asteroid impact that killed the dinosaurs 65 million years ago. As mammals, we like to think that we're pretty… superior. **The sad truth**: "Mammals coexisted with

149

dinosaurs for 150 million years but were **never** able to get beyond **little ratlike** things," says Knoll. "It was only when the dinosaurs were removed that mammals had the ecological freedom to evolve new features" (2002, 133[4]:45, emp. added).

Statements like these have routinely appeared in "factual" evolutionary articles over the past century. But, as so often is the case, when more evidence is gathered, evolutionary "facts" become outright errors. Whereas Hayden touted "the reality" of evolution and "the sad truth" that mammals in the time of the dinosaurs were "**never** able to get beyond little ratlike things" (p. 45, emp. added), three years later the fossils of a mammal "20 times larger" than what evolutionists believed to be possible, were reported to be in the same fossil beds as the

Southern short-tailed shrew

dinosaurs (see Verrengia, 2005). Another mammal discovered in the same region actually had the remains of a five-inch dinosaur **in its stomach**—proof that mammals much larger than chipmunks and rats not only lived with dinosaurs, but even ate some of them (see Hu, et al., 2005, 433:151).

One year after scientists reported the dinosaur-eating mammal, the *Associated Press, Reuters,* and a host of other news outlets disseminated stories documenting the discovery of another fossilized mammal, "in the Inner Mongolia region of China," that looked very much like a beaver (Schmid, 2006). The

creature was given the name *Castorocauda lutrasimilis* (meaning beaver tail in Latin). Its skeleton was "accompanied by fur and scale imprints and the suggestion of soft-tissue in the hind limbs" (Wilford, 2006).

What, exactly, is so interesting to the scientific community about the find? According to the "establishment," this mammal lived in China 164 million years ago, **about 100 million years before** most evolutionary scientists believed mammals filled such niches as swimming, or grew bigger than a shrew. Schmid wrote: "The discovery of a furry, beaverlike animal that lived at the same time of dinosaurs overturned **more than a century of scientific thinking about Jurassic mammals**. The find shows that the ecological role of mammals in the time of dinosaurs was far greater than previously thought" (2006, emp. added). Wilford added: "In the conventional view, the earliest mammals were small, primitive shrewlike creatures that did not begin to explore the world's varied environments until the dinosaurs died out 65 million years ago" (2006). He went on in the article to explain that the find totally upsets this conventional view.

Let's analyze what is happening here. For the last "century," science textbooks have been teaching us and our children that the mammals that lived with dinosaurs were small, about the size of a shrew. This "conventional" teaching held by the majority of the scientific establishment was impressed upon our minds in a host of memorable ways. We were treated to stories in which the characters would travel back in time to the age of the dinosaurs with no references to mammals. We have viewed museum exhibits that portray dinosaurs everywhere, with no sign of mammals. We have been shown textbook illustrations depicting dinosaurs that conspicuously leave out all mammals. Yet, one little beaver-like creature overturns all that evolutionary scientists previously thought about the coexistence of mammals and dinosaurs. If evolutionists have been blatantly wrong about the coexistence of mammals and dinosaurs, could they not be just as wrong about the coexistence of men and dinosaurs?

The aggravating thing about this situation is that in the articles reporting the find, there is no accountability for the wrong information that has been disseminated for the past century. How is it that the majority of the most brilliant scientists in the world have been off by 100 million years? And how is it that the information about shrew-like mammals, which has been taught as virtual fact in every outlet available, gets jettisoned by a single find, yet no one questions the way that such erroneous information could get passed on for so long?

It is time that critical thinkers take a long, hard look at the "conventional" beliefs of the scientific establishment. One hundred million years is a huge amount of time to brush aside with a wave of the hand. The truth is, not only are evolutionary ideas about when mammals lived wrong, but the entire system is based on

unproven assumptions, inaccurate calculations, and ridiculously exaggerated periods of millions of years (which can be modified by hundreds of millions on a whim). What new find will surface tomorrow that eradicates another 100 million years of assumed time and a century of conventional thinking?

"SOFT" DINOSAUR TISSUE?

According to evolutionists, dinosaur bones are at least 60 million years old. More and more evidence is coming to light from the fossil record, however, which casts serious suspicion on evolutionists' geologic timeta-
ble. In 2005, "paleontologists were **stunned** to find that the soft tissue of a...dinosaur was preserved within a fossil from a Tyrannosaurus rex" (Boyle, 2007, emp. added). Dr. Mary Schweitzer and her colleagues reported the find in *Science* magazine, describing the demineralized *T. rex*

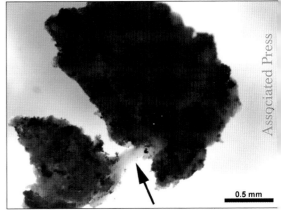

Tyrannosaurus rex bone tissue described as "soft," "fibrous," "flexible," and "resilient."

femur and tibia fragments as "highly fibrous," "flexible," and so "resilient" that "when stretched, returns to its original shape" (Schweitzer, et al., 2005, 307:1952,1953; Schweitzer, et al., 2007, 316:277). Amazingly, the researchers were even able to **squeeze** round, dark-red-to-deep-brown microscopic structures from the presumed *T. rex* blood vessels (Perkins, 2005, 167[13]:195). Scientists were shocked! "Such a thing had never been seen before" (Boyle, 2007). How could an alleged "**70-mil-**

153

lion-year-old" *Tyrannosaurus rex* bone still contain soft tissue?

For those who may chalk this up as just some anomaly that should cast no doubt upon the multi-million-year evolutionary timetable, consider

Associated Press

what *MSNBC* science editor Alan Boyle reported two years later: "Today, paleontologists are still stunned—not only to find material that looks like dinosaur cartilage, blood vessels, blood cells

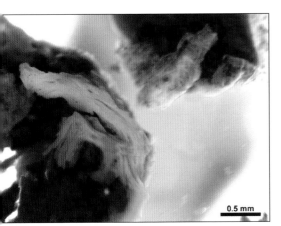

Associated Press

and bone cells, but to **see the stuff in so many different specimens**" (emp. added). Paleontologist Kristi Rogers of Macalester College said: "It's not just a fluke occurrence…. It's something that's more pervasive in the fossil record" (as quoted in Boyle). Scientists have excavated a

Tyrannosaurus and a hadrosaur from Montana, a *Titanosaurus* from Madagascar, and more samples that the famous dinosaur fossil hunter Jack Horner has uncovered in Montana, as well as Mongolia. Regarding the hadrosaur specimen found in Montana, Dr. Mary Schweitzer stated: "It's the 'freshest,' if you

will, dinosaur bone that has ever had this analysis conducted on it" (as quoted in Boyle).

Although evolutionists continue to describe such dinosaur bones as being "70 million years old," "miraculously preserved soft tissue" (Gebel, 2007) in a "growing number of tissue samples" (Boyle, 2007) around the world demands a reasonable explanation. Suggesting that these bones sat around for at least 70 million years (or 25.55 **billion** days) in "porous sandstone" (Morris, n.d.) without completely fossilizing or decomposing, literally is unbelievable. A much better, more logical explanation is that dinosaurs once lived on Earth in the not-too-distant past—only a few hundred or thousand years ago, not 60+ million years ago. If soft, flexible, resilient, highly fibrous dinosaur tissue in many different specimens will not convince the evolutionists to rethink their theories about dinosaurs and humans, what in the world would?

Carbon-14 Dating

According to evolutionary scientists, radiocarbon dating (also known as carbon-14 dating) is totally ineffective in measuring time when dealing with millions of years. In his 2000 book, *Genes, People, and Languages,* renowned Stanford University geneticist Luigi Cavalli-Sforza, in a discussion on the theory of human evolution, commented on radiocarbon dating, stating: "The most crucial dates in modern human evolution are unfortunately beyond the range of the radiocarbon method, **which has a limit of about 40,000 years**" (p. 61, emp. added). Staunch evolutionist Richard Dawkins also dealt with the limitations of radiocarbon dating a few years ago in his highly touted book, *The Blind Watchmaker.* He was even more critical of this dating method than was Cavalli-Sforza, saying:

> Different kinds of radioactive decay-based geological stopwatches run at different rates. The radiocarbon stopwatch buzzes round at a great rate, so fast that, after some thousands of years, its spring is almost wound down and the watch is no longer reliable. **It is useful for dating organic material on the archaeological/historical timescale where we are dealing in hundreds or a few thousands of years, but it is no good for the evolutionary timescale where we are dealing in millions of years** (1986, p. 226, emp. added).

Both evolutionists and creationists stand in agreement that radiocarbon dating, which can be used only to date organic (once living) samples, is totally ineffective in measuring the alleged millions or billions of years of the evolutionary timetable. [In truth, even when dating things that are relatively

young, carbon-14 dating is imperfect and based upon certain unprovable assumptions (see Major, 1993).] If radiocarbon dating can measure only items that are thousands of years old, why should evolutionists even consider using this dating method on anything that they already believe to be millions of years old? Creationists would like to see evolutionists apply this method to items believed to be millions of years old, because it might help convince evolutionists that coal, diamonds, fossils, etc. are not millions of years old, but only thousands of years old.

Consider that in recent years "readily detectable amounts of carbon-14" in materials evolutionists suppose are millions of years old "have been the rule rather than the exception" (DeYoung, 2005, p. 49). When geophysicist John Baumgardner and colleagues obtained 10 coal samples from the U.S. Department of Energy Coal Sample Bank, one of the leading radiocarbon laboratories in the world tested the samples for traces of carbon. The coal samples were analyzed using the modern accelerator mass spectrometry (AMS) method. If the coal were really many millions of years old (as evolutionists suggest), no traces of carbon-14 should have been found. "[A]ny carbon-containing materials that are truly older than 100,000 years should be 'carbon-14 dead' with C-14 levels below detection limits" (DeYoung, p. 49). But, in fact, traces of carbon-14 **were** found. "[A] residue of carbon-14 atoms was found in all ten samples.... The amounts of C-14 in coal are found to average 0.25 percent of that in the atmosphere today" (DeYoung, p. 53). Diamonds assumed to be hundreds of millions of years old were also tested—12 in all. Once again, traces of C-14 were found in every sample (see DeYoung, pp. 45-62).

In June of 1990, Hugh Miller submitted two dinosaur bone fragments to the Department of Geosciences at the University in Tucson, Arizona for carbon-14 analysis. One fragment was from an unidentified dinosaur. The other was from an *Allosaurus* excavated by James Hall near Grand Junction, Colorado in 1989. Miller submitted the samples without disclosing the identity of the bones. (Had the scientists known the samples actually were from dinosaurs, they would not have bothered dating them, since it is assumed dinosaurs lived **millions** of years ago—outside the limits of radiocarbon dating.) Interestingly, the C-14 analysis indicated that the bones were from 10,000-16,000 years old—a far cry from their alleged 60-million-year-old age (see Dahmer, et al., 1990, pp. 371-374).

What is C-14 doing in coal, diamonds, and dinosaur fossils, if these objects are really many millions of years old? Richard Dawkins declared that C-14 dating "is useful for dating organic material on the archaeological/historical timescale where we are dealing in **hundreds** or a **few thousands** of years," not millions of years (1986, p. 226, emp. added). Yet, "readily

detectable amounts of carbon-14," even in coal, diamonds, and various fossils, "have been the rule rather than the exception" in recent years (DeYoung, 2005, p. 49). Why? Evolutionists assert that the specimens in every case must have been contaminated by outside carbon. After all, everyone "knows" coal is millions of years old, right? Using C-14 dating on specimens already believed to be only hundreds or a few thousands of years old is considered acceptable. Scientists expect to find carbon in samples they perceive as young. But, if specimens believed to be millions of years old are tested (e.g., coal), and found to have carbon traces, then they "must" have been contaminated. Or so we are told.

Informed creation scientists, like members of the RATE (Radioisotopes and the Age of the Earth) team, contend that the modern "AMS measurements carefully eliminate all possible sources of carbon contamination. These include any trace of C-14 which has possibly entered the samples in recent history, or C-14 introduction during sample preparation and analysis" (DeYoung, 2005, p. 50). Whereas "unexpected carbon-14 was initially assumed to be a result of contamination…, as this problem was aggressively explored, it was realized that most of the carbon-14 was inherent to the samples being measured" (p. 49).

The fact is, significant traces of carbon have been detected in samples that "should not" contain carbon. Since evolutionists are unwilling to adjust their million/billion-year timetable, they are forced to conclude that radiocarbon dating is always faulty when it comes up with young dates (measured in hundreds or thousands of years) for assumed old specimens (supposedly

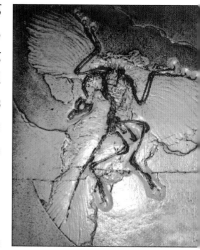

millions of years old). Do you see anything wrong with this picture? The fact is, coal, diamonds, and dinosaur fossils containing traces of carbon are no surprise. One would expect to find such if the biblical accounts of Creation and the Flood are true. [NOTE: For a discussion on radiometric dating, see chapter 8.]

ARCHAEOPTERYX

One of the most unusual birds of the past is known as *Archaeopteryx* (ark-ee-OP-tuh-riks). Even though *Archaeopteryx* [meaning "ancient" (Greek *archae*) "wing" (*pteryx*)] had feathers, and was about the size of a pigeon, controversy has surrounded this creature for a long time because it also had some features that are similar to a small dinosaur—it had teeth in its beak and claws on its wings. Because of such characteristics, you are likely to find a replica of this fossilized creature in the dinosaur section of many museums of natural history. A number of evolutionists believe that this animal either was a link between reptiles and birds, or was the "first true bird," and is allegedly proof that birds evolved from

reptiles. In their widely used high school biology text, *Life: An Introduction to Biology*, evolutionists Simpson, Pittendrigh, and Tiffany declared: "Perhaps the most famous intermediate is that between reptiles and birds...*Archaeopteryx*" (1957, p. 31). Later, in the same book, they stated: "The oldest known fossil birds (*Archaeopteryx*, "ancient wing") were still almost reptilian except in one respect: they had feathered wings" (p. 591). Evolutionists maintain that the claws and teeth of *Archaeopteryx* suggest that it had been a reptile in the past.

Actually, however, such characteristics of *Archaeopteryx* do not prove that it was the missing link between reptiles and birds. Consider that some **modern** birds have claws on their wings, and yet no one thinks of them as being missing links. The African bird known as touraco has claws on its wings, as does the hoatzin of South America when it is young. Both of these birds use their fully functional claws to grasp branches and climb trees. If you have ever seen an ostrich close up, you might have noticed that it, too, has claws on each wing and can use them if attacked. Obviously, simply because a bird in the fossil record is discovered with claws on its wings does not mean that it is a transitional fossil.

In 1993, *Science News* reported that an odd fossil

The country of Bhutan featured the hoatzin on a mailing stamp.

161

bird had been unearthed in Mongolia. It supposedly is millions of years younger than *Archaeopteryx* and, interestingly, had teeth in its beak (Monasterky, 1993, 143:245). As with the claws on the wings of *Archaeopteryx*, evolutionists cannot prove that the presence of teeth make the animal something more than a bird. What's more, consider that while most reptiles have teeth, turtles do not. And, some fish and amphibians have teeth, while other fish and amphibians have no teeth. How can evolutionists be so sure that *Archaeopteryx's* teeth make it a dinosaur-bird link? Such an assertion is based only on biased, unprovable assumptions.

Archaeopteryx also had **fully formed** feathers, just like living birds. Fossils of *Archaeopteryx* leave no hint of the animal being a half-scaly/half-feathered creature. It was not in some kind of in-between stage. Furthermore, "[e]xperts **don't know** what *Archaeopteryx's* closest [alleged–EL/KB] dinosaur ancestor looked like–fossils haven't yet been found" ("Fossil Evidence," 2007), i.e., evolutionists have been entirely unsuccessful in finding the real alleged missing link between dinosaurs and birds.

Finally, what makes the suggestion that *Archaeopteryx* was the missing link between reptiles and birds (or that it was the "first true bird") even more unbelievable is that "[a]nother bird fossil found in the desert of west Texas in 1983, *Protoavis*, is dated even earlier, 75 million years **before** *Archaeopteryx*" (DeYoung, 2000, p. 37, emp. added). Although some paleontologists have questions about the fossil remains of *Protoavis* (birds, after all, were not supposed to be around with the "earliest dinosaurs"), Dr. Chatterjee of Texas Tech University "has

pointed out, the skull of Protoavis has 23 features that are fundamentally bird-like, as are the forelimbs, the shoulders, and the hip girdle" (Harrub and Thompson, 2001). In 1991, *Science* magazine ran a story titled "Early Bird Threatens *Archaeopteryx's* Perch," wherein Alan Anderson wrote: "His [Chaterjee's–EL/KB] reconstruction also shows a flexible neck, large brain, binocular vision, and, crucially, portals running from the rear of the skull to the eye socket–a feature seen in modern birds but not dinosaurs" (253:35).

The fact is, the fossil record does not, in any way, demonstrate that dinosaurs evolved into birds. According to Scripture, God created flying animals and land animals separately in the Creation week (Genesis 1-2). The Bible indicates that birds were birds from the beginning of their existence; they were created by God on day five of the creation week. According to Genesis 1, birds were flying even before dinosaurs were formed on the following day (vs. 25). [NOTE: For more information on *Archaeopteryx* and the alleged evolution of dinosaurs to birds, see Harrub and Thompson, 2001.]

Artist's rendition of *Archaeopteryx*

CHAPTER 8

Science, Scripture, and the Age of the Earth

Since the days of Charles Darwin, it has become crystal clear that in order for evolution to have even the remotest chance of occurring, it must be given billions of years. (Of course, no amount of time could help the impossible.) In Darwin's day, many scientists thought that 20 million years would be enough time. But as scientists began to discover the intricate complexity of the Universe, it soon became evident that the time frame must be increased by billions of years. In order to "prove" that these billions of years have occurred, certain dating methods have been invented to calculate the Earth's age. If you ever took Earth Science in school, then you most likely have studied the different ways that scientists "date" the rocks and other materials of the Earth. However, what you may not have heard is that the dating methods yielding billions of years have some serious flaws.

165

RADIOMETRIC DATING

The heroes for evolutionary dating that are supposed to be able to give ages in the billions are the various radiometric dating methods. Each of these methods is based upon the decay rate of certain elements. In one method, for instance, the element uranium-238 will break down into the element lead over a period of many years. The element that breaks down (in this case, uranium-238) is called the parent element, and the element that is formed (in this case, lead) is called the daughter element. How long is this supposed to take? In the case of uranium and lead, the half-life is supposed to be 4.5 billion years. A half-life is simply the time that it takes half of a sample of the parent element to turn into the daughter element. For instance, if you have 50 ounces of uranium, then in 4.5 billion years you supposedly should have about 25 ounces of uranium and 25 ounces of lead. Therefore, if you know the rate of decay for an element, once you measure the amount of the two elements in the rock sample, simple math should give you an age for the rock. However, certain assumptions cause radiometric dating to be irreparably flawed.

Uranium

Lead

ASSUMPTION 1: THE RATE OF DECAY HAS ALWAYS BEEN THE SAME

The first major assumption inherent in radiometric dating is the idea that the parent elements have decayed in the past at the exact same rate as they are decaying today. This idea has problems, because no one alive today knows what kind of environment existed in the distant past. We cannot claim to know how fast elements decayed in the past, because we do not have any evidence to prove this idea. Consider how drastically this idea could alter the age of the Earth. Suppose you come upon a man who is cutting down trees in a forest. You watch him for an entire hour and he only cuts down one tree. Then you count the number of trees he has cut–31 in all. **If you assume** that he has been cutting trees down at the same rate all day, then you calculate that he has chopped for 31 hours. However, when you talk to the man, he informs you that, earlier in the day when his ax was sharp and his stomach filled, he was cutting down five trees an hour; only in the last hour had he slacked. With this information, you now understand that he worked

for only seven hours, not 31. Claiming that the decay rates in the past were the same as they are now is an assumption that cannot be proven and cannot be granted to those who want an age for the Earth measured in billions of years.

ASSUMPTION 2: ELEMENTS HAVE NOT BEEN AFFECTED BY OUTSIDE FORCES

Another assumption built into the radiometric dating methods is the idea that the elements have not been affected by outside forces. That means that no water has soaked through the sample and "carried away" some of the lead, or that none of the uranium had a chance to escape through pores in the rock. However, this is a huge assumption. How can a person claim that environmental forces have not affected the elements in a rock for a period of billions of years? In 4.5 billion years, could it be slightly possible that water seeped through the sample and added or subtracted some lead or uranium? Furthermore, could there be an "outside chance" that some of the uranium seeped out of pores in the rock (after all, evolutionists delight in "outside chances")? If any rock were really 4.5 billion years old, no one in this world would have a clue what had or had not gone in or out of the rock over that vast amount of time. Once again, the assumption that certain rock samples are "closed systems" simply cannot be granted.

ASSUMPTION 3: NO DAUGHTER ELEMENT EXISTED AT THE BEGINNING

To date rocks using any radiometric dating system, a person must assume that the daughter element in the sample was not present in the beginning. However, that claim cannot be proven. Who is to say that the rock did not start out with 23 grams of lead already in it? The lead could have been in the rock from the beginning. To illustrate this point, suppose you go to a swimming pool and find a hose that is pumping water into the pool at a rate of 100 gallons an hour. You discover that the pool has 3,000 gallons of water in it. You calculate that the hose must have been running for 30 hours. However, when you ask the owner of the pool how long she has been running the hose, she tells you that she has been running it for only one hour and that most of the water was already in the pool due to a heavy rain the night before. If you assumed that all the water came from the hose, your calculations would be way off–29 hours off to be exact. Assumption three, that no daughter element existed in the sample at the beginning, simply cannot be granted.

ANOTHER PROBLEM WITH RADIOMETRIC DATING

In addition to the assumptions that are built into radiometric dating, another problem is that the different radiometric methods often drastically disagree with one another. On occasion, the same sample of rock can be dated by the different methods and the dates can differ by several hundred million years. Some rocks from Hawaii that were known to have formed about two hundred years ago rendered a date of 160 million to 3 billion years when dated by the potassium-argon method (Funkhouser and Naughton, 1968, p. 4601). Another

Basalt

time, the same basalt rock in Nigeria was given a date of 95 million years when dated by the potassium-argon method and 750 million years when dated by the uranium-helium method. But what can you expect from dating methods that are based on built-in assumptions? Anything is possible!

If history is any accurate indication, other dating methods soon will be concocted that will give even older ages for the Earth. But each dating method that renders colossal numbers of years will be based on similar, unprovable assumptions. The fact that these vast ages of billions of years come from ever-oscillating dating methods manifests their inherent fallibility. There never have been billions of years available for evolution, and there never will be.

SCIENTIFIC EVIDENCE FOR A YOUNG EARTH

EARTH'S DECAYING MAGNETIC FIELD

In the core of the Earth, a huge electric current is produced that causes the Earth to produce a magnetic attraction. That magnetic attraction is what causes the arrow on a compass to point North. What does this have to do with the Earth's age? Scientists who have been studying the Earth's magnetic forces have discovered that they are getting weaker and weaker every year. Several years ago, a government report stated that the magnetic field would be gone by the year A.D. 3991 (McDonald and Gunst, 1967, pp. 1,5).

If we look at how fast the magnetic field is decaying today, and try to calculate how long it has been decaying, we learn something very interesting. If you go backward for just a few thousand years, the heat inside the Earth would have been so great that the Earth would have broken apart and cracked. One scientist, Thomas G. Barnes, indicated that, after measuring the magnetic field, the Earth could only be about 10,000 years old (Barnes, 1983). Maybe the Earth's magnetic field did not decay in the past like it is decaying today. But, if you look at how it is decaying today, like evolutionists do with other dating methods, we get a very young Earth that is only a few thousand years old.

HYDROGEN IN THE UNIVERSE

Our Universe is made up mostly of hydrogen. In nature, however, hydrogen is converted into helium. It does not convert back into hydrogen once it changes. And, scientists have not found any way that hydrogen can be produced in large amounts. If the Universe were millions or billions of years old, then all the hydrogen would have changed into helium. But that is not the case. The Universe still contains huge amounts of hydrogen. One famous astronomer by the name of Fred Hoyle saw this as a real problem. After studying it for some time, he concluded that the idea of any old age for the Universe is problematic. He even thought that this piece of evidence, along with others, might point to a Creator. He stated: "How comes it then that the universe consists almost entirely of hydrogen? If matter was infinitely old, this would be quite impossible. So we can see that the universe being what it is, the creation issue simply cannot be dodged" (Hoyle, 1960, p. 125). When we look at the Universe, we still see enormous amounts of hydrogen, which shows that the Universe cannot be billions of years old.

POPULATION STATISTICS

One of the strongest arguments for a young Earth comes from the field of human population statistics. According to historical records, the human population on Earth doubles approximately every 35 years. If you break down that figure, it represents an annual increase of 20,000 people per every million. Let's suppose that humankind started with just two

individuals (we will call them Adam and Eve for the sake of our argument). And suppose that they lived on the Earth one million years ago (some evolutionists suggest that man, in one form or another, has been on the Earth 2-3 million years). Suppose, further, that an average generation was 42 years, and that each family had an average of 2.4 children. (They probably had many more than that, but we will use a conservative estimate that would allow for at least some population growth; if a family unit had only two children, there would be zero population growth, since each parent simply would replace himself or herself, providing no net increase.)

Allowing for wars, famine, diseases, and other devastation, there would be approximately 1×10^{5000} people on the Earth today! That number is a 1 followed by 5,000 zeroes. But the entire Universe (at an estimated size of 20

billion light-years in diameter) would hold only 1×10^{100} people. Evolutionary time scales simply cannot account for the present, relatively small human population. However, using young-Earth figures (of eight people having survived the Noahic Flood), the current world population would be around 6-8 billion people. The question is—which of the two figures is almost right on target, and which could not possibly be correct? [NOTE: This brief description and calculation can be found in more complete form in Lammerts, 1971, pp.

198-205; Wysong, 1976, pp. 168-169; and Morris and Morris, 1996, pp. 317-320.]

THE BIBLE, MAN, AND THE AGE OF THE EARTH

According to evolution, man is a newcomer to planet Earth, far removed from the origin of the Universe. If the Universe was born 14 billion years ago, as many evolutionists, theistic evolutionists, and progressive creationists believe, man did not "come along" until about 13.996 billion years later. If such time were represented by one 24-hour day, and the alleged Big Bang occurred at 12:00 a.m., then man did not arrive on the scene until 11:59:58 p.m. Man's allotted time during one 24-hour day would represent a measly two seconds.

If the Bible taught, either explicitly or implicitly, that man was so far removed from the origin of the Universe, a faithful, Bible-believing Christian would have no reservations accepting the above-mentioned timeline. Just as a Christian believes that God parted the Red Sea (Exodus 14), made an iron ax head float on water (2 Kings 6:5), and raised Jesus from the dead (Matthew 28:1-8), he would need to accept that humans appeared on Earth billions of years after the beginning of Creation—**if** that was what the Bible taught. The problem for theistic evolutionists and progressive creationists is that God's Word never hints at such a timeline. In fact, it does the very opposite.

The Bible makes a clear distinction between things that took place **before** "the foundation of the world" and events that occurred **after** the "foundation of the world." Jesus prayed

to the Father on the night of His arrest and betrayal, saying, "You loved Me **before** the foundation of the world" (John 17:24, emp. added). Peter revealed in his first epistle how Jesus "was foreordained **before** the foundation of the world, but was manifest in these last times for you" (1 Peter 1:20, emp. added). Paul informed the Christians in Ephesus how God "chose us in Him **before** the foundation of the world, that we should be holy and without blame before Him in love" (Ephesians 1:4, emp. added). **Before** "God created the heavens and the earth" (Genesis 1:1), He was alive and well.

If theistic evolutionists and progressive creationists are correct, then man arrived on the scene, not **before** the foundation of the world (obviously), nor **soon after** the foundation of the world, but **eons later**–13.996 billion years later to be "precise." This theory, however, blatantly contradicts Scripture.

Jesus taught that "the blood of all the prophets…was shed **from ("since"–NASB) the foundation of the world…, from the blood of Abel** to the blood of Zechariah who perished between the altar and the temple" (Luke 11:50-51, emp. added; cf. Luke 1:70). Not only did Jesus' first-century enemies murder the prophets, but their forefathers had slain them as well, ever since the days of Abel. Observe that Jesus connected the time of one of the sons of Adam and Eve (the first couple on Earth, created on day six of Creation–Genesis 1:26-31) to the "foundation of the world." This time is contrasted with the time of a prophet named Zechariah, whom, Jesus told His enemies, "**you** murdered between the temple and the altar" (Matthew 23:35, emp. added). Zechariah was separated from the days of Abel by thousands of years. His blood was not shed near the foundation of the world; Abel's was. Certain early martyrs, including Abel, lived close enough to Creation for Jesus to say that their blood had been shed "from the foundation of the world." If man arrived on the scene billions of years after the Earth was formed, and hundreds of millions of years after various living organisms like fish, amphibians, and reptiles came into existence (as the evolutionary timeline affirms), how could Jesus' statement make any sense? Truly, man was not created eons after the foundation of the world. Rather, he has been here "from the foundation" of it.

On another occasion when Jesus' antagonists approached Him, they questioned Him about the lawfulness of divorce. Jesus responded by saying, "But **from the beginning of the creation**, God made them male and female" (Mark 10:6, emp. added). According to Genesis 1 and 2, God made Adam and Eve on the sixth day of Creation (1:26-31; 2:7,21-25). Jesus referred to this very occasion and indicated that God made them "from the beginning of the creation." Similar to the association of Abel's day with "the foundation of the world," so the forming of Adam and Eve on day six of the Creation can be considered "from the beginning of the creation."

In the epistle to the Christians in Rome, the apostle Paul also alluded to how long man has been on the Earth. He wrote: "For **since the creation of the world** His invisible attributes are clearly seen, being understood by the things that are made, even His eternal power and Godhead…" (Romans 1:20, emp. added). Who on Earth understands the eternal power and divine nature of God? Man. (NOTE: Although some might suggest that angels can understand God's invisible attributes, the context of Romans 1:18-32 clearly is referring to humans, not angels.) How long has man been aware of God and His invisible attributes? "Since the creation of the world." How, then, could man logically have been "perceiving" or "understanding" God "**since** the creation of the world" (emp. added), if he is separated from the creation of "the heavens and the earth, the sea," and so many of the animals (like trilobites, dinosaurs, and "early mammals") by millions or billions of years? Such a scenario completely contradicts Scripture.

177

WHAT ABOUT THE DAY-AGE THEORY?

Bible believers who desire to incorporate the long ages of evolutionary geology must find some way to fit billions of years into the biblical record. One popular theory concocted to add eons of time to the age of the Earth is the Day-Age Theory, which suggests that the days of Genesis 1 were not literal, twenty-four hour days, but lengthy periods of time (millions or billions of years). Is such a theory to be welcomed with open arms, or is there good reason to reject it?

The available evidence reveals several reasons why we can know that the days mentioned in Genesis 1 are the same kind of days we experience in the present age, and were not eons of time. First, whenever the Hebrew word for day (*yom*) is preceded by a numeral (in non-prophetic passages like Genesis 1), it **always** carries the meaning of a 24-hour day. The same occurs in the plural (cf. Exodus 20:11; 31:17). Just as Jonah was in the belly of the great fish for **three days** (and not 3,000 years), and just as the Israelites marched around Jericho once a day for **six days** (and not six long vast periods of time), God created everything in "six days" (Exodus 20:11; 31:17) and not over a period of six billion years.

Second, *yom* (day) is both used and defined in Genesis 1:5. The words "evening" and "morning" are used together in the Old Testament with the word *yom* over 100 times in non-prophetic passages, and each time they refer to a 24-hour day. Furthermore, if the "days" of Genesis 1:14, were "eons of time," then what were the years? The word "years" can

only be understood correctly in this context if the word "days" means a normal day.

Third, if the "days" of Genesis were not days at all, but long evolutionary periods of time, then a problem arises in the field of botany. Vegetation came into existence on the third day (Genesis 1:9-13). If each day of Genesis 1 was a long geological age composed of one period of daylight and one period of darkness, how did plant life survive millions of years of total darkness? Also, how would the plants that depend on insects for pollination have survived the supposed millions or billions of years between "day" three and "day" five (when insects were created)? The Day-Age Theory collapses under a reasonable reading of Genesis 1.

WHAT ABOUT THE GAP THEORY?

It often has been said, "The Bible is its own best commentary." When we read something that we do not understand in one section of the Bible, frequently other passages in the Scriptures will "interpret" the "unclear" sections for us. Someone questioning the identity of the "seed" of Abraham who would be a blessing to all nations (Genesis 22:18; cf. 26:4) can read Galatians 3:16 and learn that the "seed" mentioned in Genesis is Christ. If a person wanted to know what the water baptism Jesus and the apostles commanded involved, he could study Romans 6:4, Colossians 2:12, and Acts 8:38, and come to the correct conclusion that New Testament water baptism is a burial in water, and not the mere sprinkling of water on a person. Instead of approaching the Scriptures with the mindset of, "What do **I think** about…," or "What do **you think** about…," we first need to ask ourselves, "What does **the Bible** say about itself?" If there is one section of the Scriptures that we do not understand fully, we always should examine other passages in the Bible that deal with the same subject first. Such is the case when we interpret the account of Creation recorded in Genesis 1.

Some who read Genesis 1-2 have suggested, for example, that the Hebrew words translated "create" (*bara*) and "make" (*asah*) always mean entirely different things. They believe that *bara* means "to create," while *asah* means "to re-create" or "to make over." Thus, we are told that "God **created** the heavens and earth" in the beginning (vss. 1-2), and then supposedly billions of years later, He orchestrated a six-day "make over" (vss. 3-31). The problem with this theory (commonly known as the Gap Theory) is that the "explanatory notes" God has given us throughout the Old Testament concerning the events recorded in Genesis 1 reveal that the words "create" (*bara*) and "make/made" (*asah*) are used interchangeably in reference to the creation of the Universe and everything in it. They are not referring to two events separated by billions of years.

Consider Exodus 20:11: "For in six days the Lord made [*asah*] the heavens and the earth, the sea, and all that is in them, and rested the seventh day." Gap theorists contend that this verse speaks only of God's "re-forming" from something already in existence. Yet notice that the verse specifically speaks of the **heavens** and the **earth**–the very same things mentioned in Genesis 1:1. Notice also the psalmist's commentary on Genesis 1:

> Praise the Lord! Praise the Lord from the heavens; praise Him in the heights! Praise Him, all His angels; praise Him, all His hosts! Praise Him, **sun** and **moon**; praise Him, all you **stars** of light! Praise Him, you heavens of heavens, and you waters above the heavens! Let them praise the name of the Lord, for He commanded and they were **created** (Psalm 148:1-5, emp. added).

The psalmist indicated that the Sun, Moon, and stars (among other things) were **created** (*bara*). However, Genesis 1:16 states: "God **made** (*asah*) two great lights: the greater light to rule the day, and the lesser light to rule the night. He **made** (*asah*) the stars also." When we couple Genesis 1:16 with Psalm 148:1-5, the only logical conclusion that we can draw is that "to create" and "to make" are used to refer to the same event–the making of heavenly bodies on the fourth day of creation.

Consider what Nehemiah wrote concerning God's creation:

> You alone are the Lord; You have **made** (*asah*) heaven, the heaven of heavens, with all their **host**, the earth and everything on it, the seas and all that is in them, and You preserve them all. The **host of heaven** worships You (9:6, emp. added).

When Nehemiah wrote about some of the same events recorded in Psalm 148:1-5 and Genesis 1:1 [in which the word "created" (*bara*) was used], he employed the word "made" (*asah*).

After surveying the creation account, one finds that no distinction is made between God's creating (*bara*) and His making (*asah*). These words are used 15 times in the first two chapters of Genesis in reference to God's work. Genesis 1:21 states that God "created" (*bara*) the sea creatures and birds. Then in 1:25 we read where God "made" the animals of the Earth. Are we to believe that God created the birds and fish from nothing and then "refashioned" the land animals from materials he had made billions of years earlier? Preposterous! In Genesis 1:26-27 we read that God made (*asah*) man in His image. Yet, the very next verse says that He created (*bara*) him in His image. How can one assert (logically) that in these two verses "make" and "create" refer to completely different creations?

What does all of this prove, you may ask? It proves that we can know God created everything in six days—including the heavens and Earth mentioned in Genesis 1:1.

The reason that some insist on the Hebrew words *bara* and *asah* having two different meanings when referring to God's creative acts is not because it is the most logical reading of the text (especially in light of other verses in the Bible), but because they are searching for some way to fit billions of years of alleged Earth history into the Bible in order to accept the evolution-based geologic timetable.

183

Conclusion

Gap theorists and Day-Age theorists who propose that billions of years of time preceded the creation of Adam and Eve need to give serious thought to the many Bible passages that teach otherwise. The Bible is not silent regarding our origins. God Almighty created the Universe (and everything in it) simply by speaking it into existence. He said, "'Let there be light'; and there was light" (Genesis 1:3).

> By the word of the Lord the heavens were made, and all the host of them by the breath of His mouth… Let all the earth fear the Lord; let all the inhabitants of the world stand in awe of Him. For He spoke, and it was done; He commanded, and it stood fast (Psalm 33:6,8-9, emp. added).

The same God Who turned water into wine in only a moment of time (without dependence on time-laden naturalistic processes like photosynthesis; John 2:1-11), "the God Who does wonders" (Psalm 77:14), spoke the Universe into existence in six days.

Had God chosen to do so, He could have spent six billion years, six million years, or six thousand years creating the world. Had He given **any** indication in His Word that lengthy amounts of time—millions or billions of years—were used in order for naturalistic processes to take over during Creation, we could understand why Christians would believe such. However, God has done the very opposite. First, He revealed that the heavens and the Earth are the effects of supernatural causes (thus contradicting the General Theory of Evolution). Second, He gave us the sequence of events that took place,

which further contradicts evolutionary theory (e.g., the Sun and stars were created after the Earth, not before–Genesis 1:14-19; birds were created before dinosaurs, not after–Genesis 1:20-23). What's more, He told us **exactly** how long He spent creating. The first chapter of Genesis reveals that from the creation of the heavens and the Earth to the creation of man, He spent six days. On two occasions in the very next book of the Bible, He reminds us that the Creation took place, not over six eons of time, but over a period of six days: "For in six days the Lord made the heavens and the earth, the sea, and all that is in them, and rested the seventh day" (Exodus 20:11; cf. 31:17). He then further impressed on Bible readers that man is not 14 billion years younger than the origin of the Universe, by referring to him as being on the Earth (1) "from the **beginning** of the creation" (Mark 10:6), (2) "**since** the creation of the world" (Romans 1:20), and (3) "**from** the foundation of the world" (Luke 11:50).

If God **did** create everything in six literal days, and expected us to believe such, what else would He have needed to say than what He said? How much clearer would He have needed to make it? And, if it does not matter what we think about the subject, why did He reveal to us the sequence of events to begin with?

Truly, just as God has spoken clearly on a number of subjects that various "believers" have distorted (e.g., the worldwide Noahic Flood, the return of Christ, etc.), the Bible plainly teaches that God, by the word of His mouth, spoke the Universe and everything in it into existence in six days.

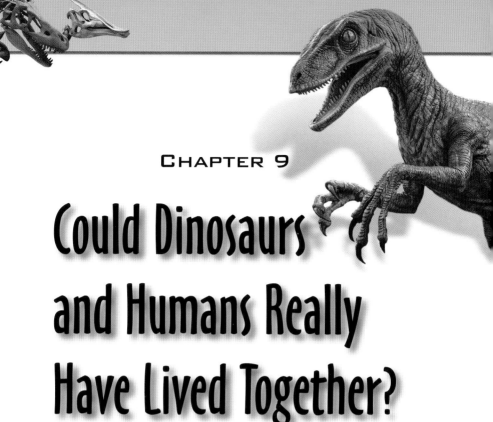

CHAPTER 9

Could Dinosaurs and Humans Really Have Lived Together?

Why is it so difficult for people to accept that dinosaurs and humans once lived together? No doubt one of the reasons is due to the fact that for many years, we have been inundated with information—on television, in books, in classrooms, in movies, in magazines, and on all sorts of paraphernalia—suggesting that dinosaurs and humans are separated by 60+ million years of geologic time. Thus, evolutionary scientists (and those who accept their timeline) have constructed a barrier that must be broken down in order to get people to consider the coexistence of dinosaurs and humans.

A second reason why people are uneasy about the idea of dinosaurs and humans living contemporaneously on Earth (and one that we want to explore further in this chapter) is

187

that in the 21ˢᵗ century, mankind is accustomed to thinking that almost all dinosaurs were enormous killing machines with which people simply could not have lived. John Clayton has proposed, for example: (1) "It is ludicrous to suggest that man cohabited with the dinosaurs in an *Alley Oop* kind of world" (1991, p. 37); and (2) "Man could not have lived in a world full

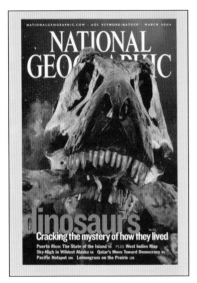

of dinosaurs, so by the time God created Adam the dinosaurs were gone" (1990, p. 14). People apparently seem to think that dinosaurs would have killed all of the humans by biting them in half with their super-sized teeth, or by hunting them down and cutting them open with five-inch long, sickle-like claws. People think that the large plant eaters would have crushed humans with their massive feet, or smashed them with their huge tails. Humans are just too small, dumb, and scrawny to have lived during the time of the dinosaurs. At least that seems to be the way evolutionary scientists, moviemakers, book writers, and magazine editors, like those from *National Geographic*, portray these "terrible lizards."

Truly, dinosaurs were remarkable creatures. Some were extremely large. Others were smaller, but with sharp teeth and long claws. Some had big heads, some had giant tails, and some had both. Others were covered with spikes or armored plates. People, in general, seem to think of them as being almost invincible—animals that lived during a time in which

man simply could not have survived. They would have been unapproachable, and certainly, untamable. Right? Just how is it that creationists can reasonably believe that dinosaurs and humans once lived on this Earth together at the same time?

EXTRAORDINARY EXTANT CREATURES

Most people today, it seems, are constantly on the go. Whether man or woman, young or old, with children or without, we (especially in America) are a busy people. Time seems to leave us before we realize we had it. We go to the office, attend meetings, and learn what we are told. We work hard, and we play hard. But how often do people step back from the hustle and bustle of life, take a deep breath, and think outside of the proverbial box? Consider the topic of dinosaurs. Rather than thinking critically about the possibility of humans and dinosaurs coexisting on Earth at one time in the past, most students are content to swallow everything a high school teacher or college professor tells them about the "wild world" of dinosaurs. In the classrooms of evolutionary scientists, thinking outside the "evolutionary box" (e.g., questioning whether it is logical to believe in the cohabitation of dinosaurs and humans) is unacceptable conduct.

The truth is, humans live in a world that is home to many incredible creatures. Numerous large animals,

189

some of which are very intimidating, cohabit this Earth with humanity, and have for thousands of years. Man generally shies away from some of these animals. Others, however, he has been able to nurture and tame.

Komodo Dragons are the world's largest lizards. They can grow to be 10 feet long (almost twice the length of an average human) and can weigh as much as 200 pounds. Still, their short, stocky legs can carry them 15 miles per hour (as fast as most dogs run). After stalking and killing deer, wild boar, and other prey, they devour their dinner in a matter of minutes. Furthermore, these amazing creatures

can consume up to 80% of their own weight. A **100**-pound Komodo can eat **80** pounds of food in one meal! And, as if that is not enough "bad news" about an animal with which we share this planet, millions of deadly bacteria grow inside its mouth, and make any bite poisonous and potentially fatal. Yet despite its size, sharp teeth, speed, power, poison, and digestive habits, neither this animal, nor any other large reptile (e.g., the anaconda), has kept man from flourishing on Earth.

While continuing to think outside of the "dangerous dinosaur" box, consider the world's largest land animal with which we share the Earth today–the imperial elephant. With somewhat amusing features (such as long "noses" and big ears), these

awesome animals can reach weights of up to **11 tons** (22,000 pounds!). One elephant easily could kill a man just by stepping on him with one foot, or by striking him with its powerful trunk. Yet, for thousands of years, humans have been known to live with, and even tame, these massive beasts. Over 2,200 years ago, the empire of Carthage, led by its infamous general, Hannibal, used tame African elephants to cross the Swiss Alps and battle the Romans. Today, many elephants still are being controlled by man. Tamed elephants are used in various Asian countries in religious ceremonies, or to do physical labor like hauling lumber or transporting people from place to place. Elephants also are frequently seen performing at circuses. Amazing, is it not, that humans

have trained these creatures, which can outweigh them by as much as 20,000 pounds, to perform some of the same tricks we train dogs to perform?

Humans have been able to live alongside elephants for thousands of years. Some humans and elephants even have become very good "friends." Why, then, is it so hard for people to think of humans living together with some of the large dinosaurs? Yes, some dinosaurs like *Brachiosaurus* grew to be about four times larger than the largest elephants. Surely we would all agree, however, that if man can work, play, and go to battle alongside (or on top of!) elephants, it certainly is not absurd to think that humans did similar things with certain dinosaurs—especially when you consider that the average dinosaur (about the size of a large cow—see Horner and Lessem, 1993, p. 124) was reasonably smaller than the average elephant.

The bald eagle is one of the largest birds of prey in the world. It can weigh nearly 14 pounds and have a wingspan more than eight feet. Its curved, strong beak and "needle-sharp claws" ("Bald Eagle," 2007) aid it in catching all sorts of prey, from fish to reptiles to mammals. In 2002, CNN reported how an eagle in Madison, Maine swooped down, snatched a 13-pound dachshund from the ground, and carried it about 300 feet before letting it go (Hatcher). Though bald eagles can

be intimidating predators, even growing to be larger than some of the extinct dinosaur-like, flying reptiles, they have repeatedly been captured and tamed by man. In Auburn, Alabama, just before every Auburn University home football game, a trained bald eagle (or golden eagle) flies around the stadium. A large, bold, powerful, intimidating bird of prey swooping down among 85,000 people—fans describe the scene as breathtaking.

Whales are the largest animals of which we are aware that have ever existed on Earth—larger than any shark, elephant, or dinosaur. Blue whales have been known to weigh as much

Blue Whale

as 400,000 pounds (200 tons!), possess a heart the size of a Volkswagen Beetle, and have a tongue large enough to hold 50 people. Yet, humans have hunted many species of whales for centuries. Furthermore, whale researchers and photographers have been able to get close enough to touch these massive creatures in the open ocean.

Killer whales (also called orcas) are another one of God's magnificent creatures with which we live on the Earth. Orcas are one of the oceans' fiercest predators, able even to kill much larger whales, including blue whales, when swimming in packs (referred to as "pods"). They hunt so well that very few animals can escape their predatory practices. Orcas eat hundreds of thousands of pounds of mammal and fish meat every year. Seals, sea lions, walruses, otters, polar bears, and even a moose have all been found in the stomachs of these ferocious creatures.

Amazingly, these incredible "killing machines" (weighing

up to 11,000 pounds!) can be captured, tamed, and trained to do all sorts of things. The famous orcas living at Sea World in Orlando, Florida, occasionally take their trainers for rides on their backs. Trainers of orcas even have been known to stick their heads inside the whales' mouths (which usually hold about 40-56 large, 3-inch-long teeth) without fear of being bitten.

How can a mere 150-pound man teach an 8,000-pound whale to jump hurdles, ring bells, and perform other tricks—without being harmed? The answer is found in the fact that God made man in His own image, and gave him the ability to have dominance over the lower creation. As early as Genesis chapter 1 we read:

Then God said, "Let Us make man in Our image, according to Our likeness; let them have **dominion** over the fish of the sea, over the birds of the air, and over the cattle, over all the earth and over every creeping thing that creeps on the earth." So God created man in His own image; in the image of God He created him; male and female He created them. Then God blessed them, and God said to them, "Be fruitful and multiply; fill the earth and **subdue** it; have **dominion** over the fish of the sea, over the birds of the air, and over every living thing that moves on the earth" (1:26-28, emp. added).

Regarding this supremacy that God gave to humans over His creation, the psalmist added:

> What is man that You are mindful of him, and the son of man that You visit him? For You have made him a little lower than the angels, and You have crowned him with glory and honor. You have made him to have **dominion** over the works of Your hands; **You have put all things under his feet**, all sheep and oxen—even the beasts of the field, the birds of the air, and the fish of the sea that pass through the paths of the seas. O Lord, our Lord, how excellent is Your name in all the earth! (8:4-9, emp. added).

The reason man can tame and/or live with even the largest and most vicious creatures on Earth is because God created man higher than the animals, and gave him the ability to "subdue" them and have "dominion" over them. James wrote: "For every kind of beast and bird, of reptile and creature

of the sea, is tamed and has been tamed by mankind" (3:7). If man, in the 21st century, can live with (and tame) such amazing creatures as the Komodo Dragon, the elephant, the blue whale, and the killer whale, as well as lions ("the king of all beasts"), tigers, and bears, it should not be difficult to accept the fact that man once lived and interacted with dinosaurs. If humans today can manipulate animals that are **100 times** their own size (e.g., the elephant), that have a mouth full of 3-inch-long, dagger-like teeth (e.g.,

the killer whale), or that have claws that could be used to rip human beings apart (e.g., bears), why is it so difficult to believe that humans and dinosaurs once inhabited this Earth **at the same time**? Admittedly, many human lives likely were lost to certain species of dinosaurs for various reasons. But, for thousands of years, people also have lost their lives to animals that still inhabit the Earth today (like sharks, tigers, lions, poisonous reptiles, bears, elephants, etc.).

A Christian once called our offices upset with the fact that we commissioned an artist to depict humans and dinosaurs interacting with one another. This gentleman actually believed that dinosaurs and humans once lived together, but illustrating a children's book with paintings of humans petting dinosaurs,

197

hunting them, feeding them, etc., was supposedly too fantastical. The idea was: humans may have lived with dinosaurs in the past, but we shouldn't illustrate them interacting with each other. Consider such sentiments in light Genesis 2:19-20.

> Out of the ground, the Lord God formed every beast of the field and every bird of the air, and brought them to Adam to see what he would call them. And whatever Adam called each living creature, that was its name. So Adam gave names to all cattle, to the birds of the air, and to every beast of the field. But for Adam there was not found a helper comparable to him.

God miraculously "brought...every beast of the field" to Adam in order that he might give them names, and also that he might realize his mate had not yet been created by God. Did Adam not live alongside, interact with, and even name lions, rhinoceroses, hippopotami, elephants, etc.? And what about Noah? Bible believers who question the possibility of humans being able to cohabitate the Earth with dinosaurs and interact with them in a variety of ways should consider the types of creatures with which Noah and his family cohabited for more than 365 days while on the ark. Genesis 7:13-16 states:

Painting by Lewis Lavoie

On the very same day Noah and Noah's sons, Shem, Ham, and Japheth, and Noah's wife and the three wives of his sons with them, entered the ark–**they and every beast after its kind**, all cattle after their kind, every creeping thing that creeps on the earth after its kind, and every bird after its kind, every bird of every sort. And they went into the ark to Noah, two by two, **of all flesh in which is the breath of life**. So those that entered, male and female of all flesh, went in as God had commanded him; and the Lord shut him in (emp. added).

Representatives of **all** kinds of the land animals of the Earth were on the ark. If Christians believe that for a whole year Noah and his family could house and take care of such "intimidating" animals as bears, snakes, alligators, gorillas, lions, etc., and that these same creatures approached Adam to be named during the Creation week, why does it seem "fantastical" to illustrate ancient peoples (including Adam and Noah) together with dinosaurs? The reservations people have, no doubt, are due in large part to inaccurate or unprovable evolutionary propaganda.

Conclusion

It is very unpopular to teach that mankind once coexisted with dinosaurs. The average person has been programmed by his or her environment to think that humans and dinosaurs never could have lived together. Not only are we told that dinosaurs became extinct over 60 million years ago, but the mindset of most people seems to be that even if this alleged 60-million-year gap of time did not exist, these creatures would have been far too dangerous for us to exist along with them. Even many Christians have a difficult time accepting the idea of humans and dinosaurs cohabiting the Earth at the same time. For some reason, when these Christians read the Creation account or rehearse the story of Noah and the Flood, they rarely consider these accounts in light of the many kinds of animals that have since become extinct.

Draw a human standing next to a dinosaur (except for cartoonish purposes), and prepare to be ridiculed. Draw a human riding a small dinosaur, and you likely will be labeled eccentric. Few people seem to care that ancient art depicts Indians riding these creatures, or that an ancient Chinese writing mentions one ancient emperor who raised a dragon in his palace. Even many "Bible believers" seem to dismiss the historical and biblical evidence of humans and dinosaurs living at the same time and within close proximity to each other. But

"Prelude to the Fair"
by Lewis Lavoie

draw a picture of a man riding on the back of a 20,000-pound elephant, and no one has a problem with it. Write an article about the woman you saw at Sea World riding on the back of an 8,000 pound killer whale, or about how she stuck her head inside the whale's massive mouth, and everyone understands these stories as being acceptable observations of reality. Tell a friend about the man at the circus who has tamed lions, tigers, and bears, and that is nothing but old news. Just refrain from telling people about the evidence for man's coexistence with dinosaurs, because "that is absurd"—or so we are told.

If man can tame many types of dangerous and ferocious animals that live on Earth today, why is it so difficult to think of man being capable of surviving alongside dinosaurs? Ancient man was able to build pyramids that stood nearly 500 feet high. He constructed the Great Pyramid with over two million blocks of stone that had to be cut, transported, and assembled to create the almost six-million-ton structure. To this day, modern man still does not know exactly how the Egyptians built these great pyramids. More than one thousand years before astronomers discovered that the length of a year was precisely 365.2422 days, ancient man (without any help from computers or modern measuring devices) calculated the length of a year as 365.2420 days long. He also figured the orbit of Venus to be 584 days, when current science shows it at 583.92 days. Our early forefathers were capable of tunneling through rock in order to mine precious metals from deep within the Earth (Job 28). Humans formed tools out of bronze and iron (Genesis 4:22). And a man named Noah even built an ark thousands of years ago that was larger than many ships of today (Genesis 6-8).

Our forefathers were not the ignorant, unlearned nitwits that many evolutionists today make them out to be. Rather, our ancestors were intelligent individuals who were more than capable of surviving alongside the large reptiles of the past. Like all humans, our forefathers were made in the image of God, and given dominion "over every living thing that moves on the earth" (Genesis 1:28)–including the dinosaurs. It is time for Christians everywhere to allow the Bible and common sense to have more influence on their thinking about the past than evolutionary theory.

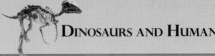

"Behemoth"
by Lewis Lavoie

203

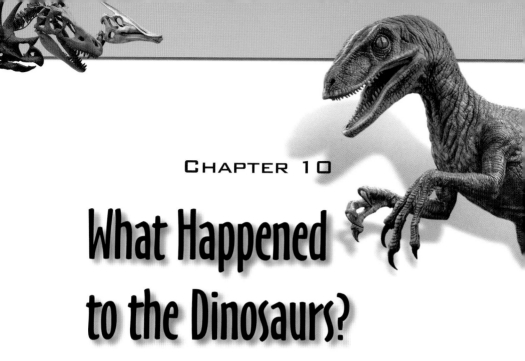

What Happened to the Dinosaurs?

Where did the dinosaurs go? This question has stumped the scientific community for decades. The question is extremely difficult because it appears that most dinosaurs (whose bones fossilized) died out in a sudden, catastrophic event. In *The Scientific American Book of Dinosaurs*, Walter Alvarez and Frank Asaro wrote: "About 65 million years ago, something killed half of all the life on the Earth. This sensational crime wiped out the dinosaurs" (2000, p. 346). Dewey McLean suggested: "Sixty-five million years ago, some phenomenon triggered **mass extinctions** on the lands and in the oceans so profound that they define the geological boundary between the older Mesozoic Era, often called the 'Age of Reptiles,' and the modern Cenozoic Era, the 'Age of Mammals'…. This mass extinction is usually referred to as the K-T extinctions" (1995, emp. added). [NOTE: Though we completely disagree with the millions-of-years timeframe suggested by Alvarez, Asaro, McLean, and others, we include their quotes simply to show that most scientists admit that a major catastrophe killed many dinosaurs in the past. We also disagree that this catastrophe caused the **extinction** of the dinosaurs, due to the fact that evidence is available which verifies that dinosaurs lived with humans after the "phenomenon" in question (see chapters 2-6).]

The perplexing mass destruction of the majority of dinosaurs remains "one of the greatest mysteries in all science" (McLean, 1995). A host of theories attempt to explain the extinction of dinosaurs. In his book *Walking with Dinosaurs*, Tim Haines noted: "There have been over 80 theories suggested to explain the demise of the dinosaurs. These include plague, constipation, mammals eating their eggs, racial senility, a nearby explosion of a supernova, and being hunted by aliens" (1999, p. 281). Dr. David Norman, one-time head of Paleontology at the Nature Conservancy Council, similarly mentioned several theories in his book on dinosaurs (1991, pp. 147-159). He called one of the theories "racial senescence" or "world-weariness." He explained that this theory suggests that dinosaurs simply had lived long enough and it was time for them to "slump into decline" and disappear. Dr. Norman then listed several other alleged causes of dinosaur extinction: slipped disc in the backbone; hormonal disorders; too much body heat; "malformations of their bone during growth; or progressive diminishing brain size resulting in death through stupidity and inability to cope with change" (p. 147). Norman continued to list theories such as massive disease, parasite infestation, overcrowding, overkill by carnivores, and a rather odd idea that caterpillars evolved at a rapid rate, stripped

the leaves off trees and depleted the food supply. Norman then listed "catastrophic" theories, such as a huge comet striking the Earth and poisoning the dinosaurs because of a large amount of cyanide contained in the comet's nose, or massive volcanic activity caused by depletion of the ozone layer (pp. 149-150). Norman also mentioned one scientist's theory that dinosaurs were blinded by monstrous cataracts caused by overexposure to ultraviolet light (p. 150).

Generally speaking, the most popularly held evolutionary view of dinosaur extinction was put forth by Luis and Walter Alvarez. In an essay co-authored with Frank Asaro, Walter Alvarez suggested that a huge, six-mile-wide asteroid crashed into the Earth and caused catastrophic, global devasta-

tion. He and Asaro wrote: "A 6-mile-diameter asteroid moving at more than 22,000 miles an hour would ram a huge hole in the atmosphere. When it hit the ground, its kinetic energy would be converted to heat in a nonnuclear explosion 10,000 times as strong as the total world arsenal of nuclear weapons" (2000, p. 350). The authors detailed many of the suggested effects of such a huge explosion. They noted that such an explosion would send enormous amounts of dust and water vapor into the atmosphere. This atmospheric contamination would result in virtually total darkness for months, and "[f]ood chains everywhere would collapse. The darkness would also produce extremely cold temperatures, a condition termed 'impact winter'" (p. 351). After this "impact winter," it is proposed that greenhouse gases such as carbon dioxide caused "a subsequent period of extreme heat that would have killed many of the dinosaurs that lived through the extreme cold" (p. 351). Add to that the heavy acid rain possibly caused by the impact, plus the idea that more asteroids may have hit the Earth, and the devastation becomes almost indescribable. In their concluding remarks, Alvarez and Asaro stated: "As detectives attempting to unravel this 65-million-year-old mystery, we find ourselves pausing from time to time to reflect that we owe our very existence as thinking beings to the impact that destroyed the dinosaurs" (p. 357).

Perhaps the second most popular evolutionary theory for dinosaur extinction is the volcano-greenhouse theory. This theory, proposed by Dewey McLean, suggests that extensive volcanic activity, focused in an area known as the Deccan Traps in India, brought about the end of the dinosaurs. The extent of volcanic activity was so great that lava flows supposedly covered the Deccan Traps area for an estimated 2.6 million square kilometers. Today, the area is still covered by about 500,000 square kilometers of lava flows. In some places, the flows are a mile and a half thick (McLean, 1995). The massive volcanic activity supposedly introduced huge amounts of water vapor and carbon dioxide into Earth's atmosphere.

These greenhouse gases allegedly trapped heat from the Sun, causing the Earth's atmosphere to heat up. According to McLean, the intense heat generated by the greenhouse gas caused "environmental heat-induced reduction of blood flow to the uterine tract, that damages and kills embryos within their mothers" (1995). Basically, the Earth got so hot that the reptiles could no longer reproduce. Still, concerning the volcano-greenhouse theory and asteroid impact theory, McLean stated: "Today, after more than 20 years of often rancorous public debate, and intense efforts by scientists who have collected a huge geobiological data base, neither theory has emerged as victorous [sic].... For now, each theory remains but a theoretical framework for future research" (1995).

The problem with all such theories is that they fall short of adequately explaining **all** the data. For example, no one knows why the effects of an asteroid striking the Earth would kill

every dinosaur but leave many other forms of life unharmed. Why did the asteroid not kill other reptiles such as turtles and alligators? What's more, nothing in the fossil record supports the death of all dinosaurs at once. Though many dinosaurs are found in fossil "graveyards" throughout the world, the evidence also shows that some lived at a later time. Evolutionist Tim Haines admitted: "No single doomsday theory fits all the evidence…" (1999, p. 281). Haines is only partially right, however; no theory based on false, evolutionary assumptions fits all data. The asteroid impact theory, volcano-greenhouse theory, caterpillar theory, constipation theory, etc., cannot explain why the reptilian dinosaurs died, but crocodiles, turtles, and other reptiles lived. They cannot account for the fact that sharks and other marine fish

and reptiles survived the event, but marine reptiles such as plesiosaurs died. As Norman noted: "The curious nature of this mass extinction is not only that it was widespread in groups that it affected, but it was also selective" (1991, p. 147). Norman's term "curious" simply means that no prevalent evolutionary theory explains it.

THE GLOBAL FLOOD

One theory pertaining to dinosaur extinction fits the available data better than any other proposed explanation: the global Flood of Noah's day. Since one of the major facts of dinosaur destruction is that most major dinosaur fossil graveyards were caused by huge amounts of water, the theory that most dinosaurs died during the worldwide Flood is the best explanation for the mass destruction of dinosaurs.

GRAVEYARDS ASSOCIATED WITH FLOODING

The Dinosaur National Monument fossil quarry is one of the largest fossil repositories in the world, where over 1,600 fossilized dinosaur bones are buried ("Dinosaur National Monument," 2004). Built around the major rock face that contains the fossils is a museum, which offers interesting information about the early discovery of the site in 1909. Like almost every federally funded dinosaur exhibit, the Dinosaur National Monument also propagates the standard evolutionary refrain that the dinosaurs lived millions of years ago. One intriguing thing about this monument is its explanation regarding the cause of its huge fossil graveyard. The wall opposite the rock face contains a large painted mural. This mural shows various dinosaurs wading through deep water. Under the mural, a placard contains the following information:

> After a seasonal flood: This scene of 145 million years ago is based on clues found in the rock face behind you.
>
> Carcasses brought downstream by the fast-moving, muddy water were washed onto a sandbar. Some were buried completely by tons of sand — their bones preserved in a near-perfect state. The bones of others, closer to the surface, were jumbled and damaged by scavengers and moving water.

On the wall opposite the fossils at the Dinosaur National Monument fossil quarry, a large painting shows a picture of what scientists think caused the fossils to form. Notice that the writing displayed near the picture suggests that the fossils formed during a flood. We have outlined the words in the paragraph that explain the scenario. While the comments on the millions of years is incorrect, the idea that a flood caused the fossils fits perfectly with the biblical idea of Noah's Flood.

"After a **seasonal flood**: This scene of 145 million years ago is based on clues found in the rock face behind you. Carcasses brought downstream by the fast-moving, muddy water were washed onto a sandbar. Some were buried completely by tons of sand–their bones preserved in a nearly perfect state" (emp. added).

Interesting, is it not, that such a huge fossil graveyard is said to have occurred because of a "seasonal flood." Further research has shown that many

fossil finds are explained using a seasonal, regional, or flash-flood scenario. In November 1999, University of Chicago paleontologist Paul Sereno uncovered a 65-foot-long dinosaur called *Jabaria*. This skeleton was almost 95% complete. What was the explanation for its burial? "It looks as though the dinosaurs may have been caught in an ancient **flash flood** and buried quickly" ("Dinosaur Articles…," 1999, emp. added). Robert Sanders, in an article copyrighted by the University of California, described a huge pterosaur graveyard by noting: "The fossil bones were found strewn throughout an ancient flood deposit in Chile's Atacama desert, suggesting that they were animals or corpses caught up in a **flood** perhaps 110 million years ago at the beginning of the Cretaceous period" (1995, emp. added).

A BBC article discussing the series "Walking with Dinosaurs" explains that much of the information for the first episode of the series came from a fossil find called the Ghost Ranch, located near Abaquiu, New Mexico. The article describes this site as one of the richest fossil finds in the world. Why were so many dinosaurs buried suddenly? "Palaeontologists believe that the collection of fossils was the result of a mass death around a dwindling water resource during a drought. Before the bodies of the animals were eaten by scavengers, a **flash flood** buried them in muddy sediments where they were preserved" ("Dig Deeper," n.d., emp. added).

In the Fall of 2007, a massive fossil bed was uncovered in an area known as Lo Hueco, in Spain. The fossil bed contained at least 8,000 fossils and bones from an estimated 100

Titanosauruses, as well as several other dinosaur species (Catan, 2007). What caused such massive burial? Fernando Escasco, a paleontologist at Cuenca's science museum, said that the animals were probably washed into the fossil bed by **"heavy flooding"** (De Elvira, 2007, emp. added).

THE GLOBAL FLOOD OF NOAH'S DAY

How interesting to learn that evolutionists explain many of the largest dinosaur graveyards in the world as having been caused by a flood (though they are quick to include words such as "seasonal," "flash," "regional," and the like). It is important to recognize that any other theory of massive dinosaur destruction, besides the global Flood of Noah's day, must still somehow propose that great amounts of water directly caused many of the dinosaur graveyards around the world. In truth, the global Flood (as recorded in Genesis 6-8) provides an excellent explanation for many (if not all) such graveyards around the world. The Bible explains that "all the fountains of the great deep were broken up, and the windows of heaven were opened. And the rain was on the earth forty

Painting by Lewis Lavoie

Painting by Lewis Lavoie

days and forty nights" (Genesis 7:11-12). Furthermore, "**all** the high hills under the **whole** heaven were covered" (Genesis 7:19, emp. added). During that year-long Flood, countless thousands of dinosaurs would have drowned and been buried quickly in muddy deposits around the world. It is reasonable to conclude that these dinosaur burial grounds became the well-known fossilized graveyards scientists have discovered around the world.

HISTORICAL EVIDENCE FOR THE FLOOD

Aside from biblical testimony of a catastrophic, worldwide flood, historical evidence also exists. Similar to the ubiquitous nature of dragon legends, anthropologists who study legends and folktales from different geographical locations and cultures consistently have reported Noahic-like flood stories. Legends have surfaced in hundreds of cultures throughout the world that tell of a huge, calamitous flood that destroyed most of mankind, and that was survived by only a few individuals and animals. Although most historians who have studied this matter estimate that these legends number above 200, according to evolutionary geologist Robert Schoch, "Noah is but one tale in a worldwide collection of at least **500 flood myths**, which are the most widespread of all ancient myths and therefore can be considered among the oldest" (2003, p. 249, emp. added). Schoch went on to observe: "Narratives of a massive inundation are found all over the world.... Stories of a great deluge are found on every inhabited continent and among a great many different language and culture groups" (pp. 103,249).

Over a century ago, Canadian geologist Sir William Dawson wrote about how the record of the Flood "is preserved in some of the oldest historical documents of several distinct races of men, and is indirectly corroborated by the whole tenor of the early history of most of the civilized races" (1895, pp. 4ff.). Legends have been reported from nations such as China, Babylon, Mexico, Egypt, Sudan, Syria, Persia, India, Norway, Wales, Ireland, Indonesia, Romania, etc.–composing a list that could go on for many pages (see Perloff, 1999, p. 167). Although the vast number of such legends is surprising, the uniformity of much of their content is equally amazing. James Perloff noted:

Painting by Lewis Lavoie

In 95 percent of the more than two hundred flood legends, the flood was worldwide; in 88 percent, a certain family was favored; in 70 percent, survival was by means of a boat; in 67 percent, animals were also saved; in 66 percent, the flood was due to the wickedness of man; in 66 percent, the survivors had been forewarned; in 57 percent, they ended up on a mountain; in 35 percent, birds were sent out from the boat; and in 9 percent, exactly eight people were spared (p. 168).

217

What is the significance of the various flood legends? The answer is obvious: (1) we have well over 200 flood legends that tell of a great flood (and possibly more than 500–Schoch, p. 249); (2) many of the legends come from different ages and civilizations that could not possibly have copied similar legends; (3) the legends were recorded long before any missionaries arrived to relate the Genesis account of Noah. The reasonable conclusion is that in the distant past, a colossal flood forever affected the history of all civilizations. As Dawson noted more than a century ago: "[W]e know now that the Deluge of Noah is not mere myth or fancy of primitive man or solely a doctrine of the Hebrew Scriptures.... [N]o historical event, ancient or modern, can be more firmly established as matter of fact than this" (1895, pp. 4ff.).

DID SOME DINOSAURS SURVIVE THE FLOOD?

Since much historical and physical evidence indicates that humans interacted with dinosaurs as recently as hundreds or thousands of years ago (e.g., stories and rock art of dinosaurs), then it must follow that some of the dinosaurs survived the Flood. What's more, since the only dry area on the globe during the Flood was on Noah's ark (Genesis 7:23), dinosaurs must have accompanied Noah and his family on the ark. Questions arise, however, as to how pairs of huge dinosaurs, some growing to lengths of over 120 feet, weighing more than 110 tons, could have been housed on the ark. First, it is important to remember that the ark was a huge vessel–300 cubits long, 50 cubits wide,

and 30 cubits high (Genesis 6:15). The word "cubit" comes from a Hebrew word meaning "forearm," because the Hebrews used their forearm in determining the length of a cubit. Generally, a cubit was the distance from the elbow to the tip of the middle finger (cf. Free and Vos, 1992, p. 182). According to our own measurements, a cubit would be about 18-20 inches. Thus, the ark was approximately 450 feet long (one-and-a-half football fields!), 75 feet wide, and 45 feet tall. For a long time, it was the largest seagoing vessel ever recorded.

The ark would have had a total floor area of about 100,000 square feet–the equivalent of slightly more than 20 standard basketball courts! And its total volume would have been roughly 1.5 million cubic feet. To help readers get a better idea of just how large the ark really was, John Whitcomb urged people to "imagine waiting at a railroad crossing while 10 freight trains, each pulling 52 boxcars, move slowly by, one after another" (1973, p. 23). Now imagine putting all of those boxcars into the ark. Whitcomb noted that the space available inside the ark would have held **520 modern railroad boxcars**! (p. 23).

To some, the idea of dinosaurs on the ark seems absurd. However, it is not so hard to accept the idea of dinosaurs on the ark after considering the subject carefully. First, remember that God was the Creator of all animals, and He knew exactly how big the ark needed to be in order to house all different kinds of land-living animals. Second, contrary to popular belief, not all dinosaurs were massive. According to the famous evolutionary dinosaur fossil-hunter John Horner, the average dinosaur was only about the size of a large cow (see Horner and Lessem, 1993, p. 124). Many dinosaurs were only a few feet tall–even as full-grown adults. Some were as small as chickens. Third, God may have allowed Noah to take baby dinosaurs into the ark, instead of those that were full grown. That allowance certainly would have saved space and reduced the amount of necessary food. The largest fossil dinosaur eggs indicate that a 40-foot-long dinosaur laid eggs that were less than a foot in diameter (see "Dinosaur Reproduction," 2007). As hatchlings, even the largest dinosaurs were no bigger than an average house pet. Young dinosaurs on the ark would have needed no more space than the average dog.

WHAT CAUSED THE DINOSAURS' ULTIMATE DEMISE?

So why did dinosaurs eventually become extinct if some survived the Flood? We do not know for sure, but one reason may be that the dinosaurs who survived the Flood on Noah's ark were unable to cope in the new world, because the climate was so different. One indication that the world was very different

Painting by Lewis Lavoie

after the Flood is that human life expectancy decreased by hundreds of years. Before the Flood, the Bible indicates that men commonly lived to be 800 and 900 years old (see Genesis 5:3-32). In fact, the grandfather of Noah, whose name was Methuselah, lived to be 969 years old (Genesis 5:27). After the Flood, however, people began dying at much younger ages. Instead of living to be 800 or 900 years old, the descendants of Noah eventually began living to be only 150 to 200 years old. For example, Abraham died at age 175 (Genesis 25:7). Although that is extremely old by today's standards, compared to the ages of people prior to the Flood, it is much younger. Many creation scientists believe that the conditions that caused man's lifespan to decrease were the same conditions that eventually (years later) drove the dinosaurs to extinction.

The last surviving dinosaurs may have become extinct for the same reason that many other animals through the years have died out—the filling of our planet with humans. It is very possible that humans hunted various kinds of dinosaurs into extinction. Certain species of tigers, bears, elephants, and hippos have all been hunted to the brink of destruction. Perhaps the same thing happened to many species of dinosaurs. Immediately after the Flood, God said to Noah and his family:

> The fear of you and the dread of you shall be on every beast of the earth, on every bird of the air, on all that move on the earth, and on all the fish of the sea. They are given into your hand. Every moving thing that lives shall be food for you. I have given you all things, even as the green herbs (Genesis 9:2-3).

Not until after the Flood do we read of God granting humans permission to hunt animals. Soon, mighty men such as Nimrod, a grandson of Ham, began hunting animals (Genesis 10:8-12). Although dinosaurs repopulated in various places throughout the world after the Flood, it could be that many eventually died at the hand of hunters. Cultures all over the world, after all, have stories of dragon slayers.

CONCLUSION

Everyone who has heard of dinosaurs likely has pondered, at one time or another, why they became extinct. The fact is, no one knows **for certain** why **all** of the dinosaurs **ultimately** died out. The worldwide Flood recorded in Genesis 6-8 undoubtedly explains adequately the presence of massive dinosaur fossil graveyards around the world, but exactly why the last dinosaur on Earth died is speculation. There are reasonable possibilities, but it is presumptuous for one to assert that he knows for sure. "What happened to the last dinosaurs?" is an interesting question, but one that we may never answer with all certainty.

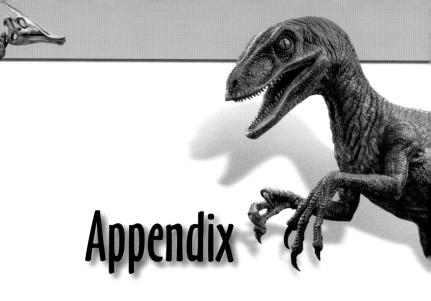

DID THE ANCIENTS BASE THEIR DINOSAUR DRAWINGS ON FOSSILS?

The presence of antiquated dinosaur carvings, figurines, and paintings around the world leaves no doubt that the ancients knew what dinosaurs looked like, long before man began excavating dinosaur bones and reconstructing their skeletons in modern times. We are convinced that the ancients' illustrations of dinosaurs serve as one of the proofs (along with the Bible and history; see chapters 2, 3, and 6) that dinosaurs and humans previously cohabited Earth. Some have suggested, however, that people living hundreds or thousands of years ago may have simply drawn pictures of dinosaurs based on fossils they found in rocks. Similar to how modern man creates illustrations, recreations, and CGI movies of dinosaurs based on the fossil record, ancient man supposedly did the same thing. Is this conclusion reasonable in light of the available evidence?

There actually are several lines of reasoning against interpreting the worldwide, antiquated dinosaur carvings as artwork made only from dinosaur fossils. First, unlike dinosaur drawings made in the 21st century, the dinosaur petroglyphs (carvings), pictographs (paintings), and figurines of antiquity are deeply embedded in a historical context of men **living with** dinosaur-like reptilian creatures often called dragons (see chapters 2 and 3). If there were no stories or references from history of men living and interacting with dinosaurs, the ancient dinosaur artwork would be less impressive testimony for the coexistence of dinosaurs and humans. If the setting of the world thousands of years ago was like it is today (where men excavate dinosaur bones, reconstruct them, and attempt to draw what they believe the creatures once looked like), then certainly the ancient artwork would be interpreted very differently. However, the historical context of hundreds and thousands of years ago was **exactly the opposite** of what it is today in reference to dinosaurs. History records how people all over the world told stories of **living** with "dragons" (i.e., dinosaurs).

> The evidence [for dragons/dinosaurs–EL/KB] is not confined to works of natural history and literature but appears in everyday chronicles of events.... And such eyewitness accounts are not derived from hearsay or anonymous rumor; they were set down by people of some standing, by kings and knights, monks and archbishops, scholars and saints (Hogarth and Clery, 1979, pp. 13-14).

If this world continues for another 1,000 years, historians in A.D. 3000 should be able to distinguish between humans drawing pictures (or making movies) of dinosaurs in A.D. 2000 (which history would clearly indicate were based upon fossil reconstructions and not cohabitation with dinosaurs), and those who made dinosaur art in A.D. 500 (and professed to live with dinosaurs).

Second, we know according to the Bible that only a few thousand years ago, man **lived with** one animal that had bones "like beams of bronze," "ribs like bars of iron" (Job 40:18), and that moved its tail "like a cedar" (40:17). Another real dinosaur/dragon-like animal on Earth in Job's day had "terrible teeth" (41:14), a powerful neck (41:22), and could breathe fire and smoke (41:18-21). What's more, if God made "the heavens and the earth, the sea, and all that is in them" during the six days of Creation (Exodus 20:11), man obviously lived with dinosaurs, as well as every other animal that has since become extinct. Thus, ancient dinosaur artwork based on **living** dinosaurs agrees with both history and the Bible.

Third, locating, excavating, reassembling, and illustrating dinosaur fossils is an extremely painstaking, complex, time-consuming process. We know of no evidence of the ancient people around the world excavating dinosaur fossils, reconstructing their skeletons, and then drawing them accurately, as scientists carefully attempt to do in the 21st century. Modern-day illustrations of dinosaurs are not done simply by illustrators going to a fossil bed and drawing what they think the dinosaur looked like. Most of the dinosaur bones discovered around the world are not even articulated (aligned in the same arrangement as in real life). According to James Powell, director of the Los Angeles County Museum of Natural History, "in spite of the intense popular and scientific interest in the dinosaurs and the well-publicized efforts of generations of dinosaur hunters, **only about 2,100** articulated dinosaur bones" exist in museums around the world (1998, p. xv, emp. added; see also Dodson, 1990, 87:7608; Lewin, 1990). Scientists have spent billions of dollars over the past 150 years persistently locating and excavating dinosaur fossils, and yet relatively few have been found aligned as they were in life. Furthermore, considering that almost half (45.3%) of all dinosaur genera are based on a **single** specimen, and 74% are represented by five specimens or less (Dodson, 1990, 87:7608), the suggestion that the ancients merely saw dinosaur fossils and drew accurate pictures of these animals seems very unreasonable. Furthermore, as previously stated, the historical context of ancient times is **not** of men **digging** up dinosaur bones, **imagining** what they looked like, and then carving them onto rock; it simply is of men carving what they saw in real life.

Fourth, ancient dinosaur artwork repeatedly is found surrounded by real-life, extant animals. As previously discussed, in the Ta Prohm temple near Siem Reap, Cambodia, the *Stegosaurus* carving is surrounded by animals still alive today, including monkeys, parrots, swans, and water buffalo. At Natural Bridges National Monument in Utah the *Apatosaurus*-like dinosaur is near a depiction of a human and a wild

goat. At the Havasupai Canyon in northern Arizona, the dinosaur-like artwork is on the same wall with an elephant, a human, and an ibex. On Bishop Bell's tomb in Carlisle, England, long-neck dinosaurs are engraved next to a bird, a pig, a fish, and a dog. The Ica stones of Peru have many other animals besides dinosaurs on them. Contrast these contexts with how modern dinosaur illustrations depict evolutionary, "scientifically accurate" settings: they show so-called "pre-historic" creatures, and not with humans, monkeys, giraffes, bears, or other large mammals, which supposedly evolved millions of years after dinosaurs became extinct. Once again, ancient dinosaur artwork is repeatedly found in a context of coexistence with humans and extant animals.

Fifth, though scientists since the early to mid-1800s have been excavating dinosaur fossils and attempting to reassemble what they think the dinosaurs looked like, so often they have been wrong in their recreations of these animals (see Potter, 2007). For example, Don Patton noted:

> When the bones of Iguanodon were discovered in the early 1800's, scientists had a very poor idea of their appearance in life. By the **late** 1800's [nearly 70 years later–EL/KB] the conception had improved considerably. **Now** we know much more. For example, ossified tendons in the tail indicate that the tail did not droop but stood out straight (n.d., emp. added).

Impressively, this scientifically accurate position is how the *Iguanodon*-like dinosaur in the Acambaro figurine collection is positioned. Consider also how scientifically accurate the sauropods **with dermal spines** were depicted in the Ica stone collection. Modern man was unaware that some (many?) sauropod dinosaurs possessed dermal spines, even though scientists had been studying the dinosaur fossils around the world for more than 150 years. This characteristic of sauropods was not learned from the fossil record until 1992. The ancient Peruvians had it right long before 1992: are we to believe they carefully examined, excavated, and reconstructed fossilized sauropod bones and skin—intricate scientific recreations that history simply does not record the ancients performing? Is it not more reasonable to conclude that man once lived with the animals that they illustrated? Modern-day paleontologists have the luxury of researching dinosaur data from all over the world and as far back as the 1820s. Our present knowledge and illustrations of dinosaurs come from their composite research. The ancients had no such comparable science, yet they still depicted dinosaurs accurately. The only logical conclusion is that the ancients actually saw living dinosaurs.

Sixth, although some have supposed that the ancients may have based their illustrations of dinosaurs on the fossil record, even various skeptics have alluded to the improbability of dinosaur art from countries like Peru, Mexico, and England being based on fossils. Evolutionist Adrienne Mayor addressed the figurines from Acambaro, and asked: "Could the reptile figures from Acambaro be amazingly accurate ancient restorations based on observations of dinosaur fossils?" Her answer: "Unlikely: the fossils in the state of Guanajuato belong to Pleistocene mastodons and horses, and not to Mesozoic dinosaurs of 250-65 million years ago" (2005, p. 337). And

what about the dinosaurs engraved on the stones from Ica? Could they be based on fossils from around that area? Mayor concluded: "No: the fossil remains of that area are of Oligocene to Pleistocene mammals, with no Cretaceous dinosaur remains" (p. 339). What about the long-neck dinosaur engraved on Bishop Bell's tomb around A.D. 1500, that even some critics admit looks "more like a quadrupedal dinosaur than any other sort of animal, past or present" ("Bishop Bell's…," 2007)? Do skeptics believe Englishmen excavated a long-neck, long-tail dinosaur in the 15th century, without leaving behind any trace or record of their paleontological work, and then had an artist engrave the animal onto Bishop Bell's tomb? Although skeptics have noted that "[t]his hypothesis…is at least possible," they admit that it is "whimsical" ("Bishop Bell's…," 2007). Whimsical indeed! Statements like these really just show that more people, even evolutionists, concede that the ancients knew what dinosaurs looked like.

Seventh, although history does not record the ancients meticulously excavating and reconstructing dinosaur bones, and then accurately drawing how these creatures looked in real life, there are hints throughout history of how, prior to modern times, people misinterpreted fossils. For example, Dr. Donald DeYoung noted that "in 1677 a large bone was found in England. It was initially attributed to the giant humans described in Genesis 6:4. However, surviving drawings of this bone look similar to a dinosaur femur" (2000, p. 39). Moreover, it has long been thought that the Cyclops legend originated from the Greeks' discovery of a young, dwarf mammoth skull, which has a nasal cavity in the middle of the skull that the ancients may have mistaken for the creature's eye socket (cf. "Meet the Original...," n.d.). No one argues about the ancients' misinterpretation of various bones and fossils. We simply are curious: where are all of the examples of the ancients accurately finding, identifying, excavating, and reconstructing dinosaur fossils?

Finally, unlike today, when scientists and scientific illustrators often recreate the skeletons of dinosaurs based on the fossil record, the ancients depicted the actual bodies of these creatures. If the ancients' knowledge of dinosaurs came from the fossil record, we would expect that they, at least occasionally, would have drawn dinosaur skeletons. Instead, we find example after example of dinosaurs as they would be seen in real life—exactly what one would expect to find if the ancients really lived with dinosaurs.

CONCLUSION

The case for the coexistence of dinosaurs and humans is cumulative. As creationists, we admittedly and unashamedly believe that the coexistence of dinosaurs and humans is based on what God's Word teaches about the creation of man and animals (Genesis 1-2; Exodus 20:11). However, the coexistence of dinosaurs and humans is also supported by history (in the form of ubiquitous, ancient dinosaur stories) and physical evidence (in the form of dinosaur artwork that the ancients in various countries around the world produced centuries ago). Truly, if man once lived with dinosaurs, such artwork, stories, and biblical testimony would be expected.

References

Alvarez, Walter and Frank Asaro (2000), "An Extraterrestrial Impact," *The Scientific American Book of Dinosaurs*, ed. Gregory Paul (New York: Byron Preiss Visual Publications).

The American Heritage Dictionary of the English Language (2000), (Boston, MA: Houghton Mifflin), fourth edition.

American Museum of Natural History (2007), Personal e-mail, November 15.

Anderson, Alan (1991), "Early Bird Threatens *Archaeopteryx's* Perch," *Science,* 253:35, July 5.

Anderson, Francis I. (1974), *Job* (Downers Grove, IL: InterVarsity Press).

Anderson, I. (1983), "Humanoid Collarbone Exposed as Dolphin's Rib," *New Scientist,* April 28.

Angier, Natalie (1985), "Drafting the Bombardier Beetle," *TIME,* February 25.

Bakker, Robert, et al. (2006), "Dracorex Hogwartsia, N. Gen., N. Sp., A Spiked, Flat-headed Pachycephalosaurid Dinosaur from the Upper Cretaceous Hell Creek Formation of South Dakota," *New Mexico Museum of Natural History and Science,* Bulletin 35, [On-line], URL: http://www.childrensmuseum.org/dinosphere/draco_rex/dracorex_hogwartsia.pdf.

"Bald Eagle" (2007), *MSN Encarta,* [On-line], URL: http://encarta.msn.com/encyclopedia_701879374/Bald_Eagle.html.

Barnes, F.A. and Michaelene Pendleton (1979), *Canyon Country Prehistoric Indians: Their Cultures, Ruins, Artifacts and Rock Art* (Salt Lake City, NV: Wasatch Publishers).

Barnes, Thomas G. (1983), *Origin and Destiny of the Earth's Magnetic Field* (ElCajon,CA:Institute for CreationResearch), revised edition.

Bates, Roy (2002), *Chinese Dragons* (Oxford: University Press).

Begun, David (2004), "The Earliest Hominins–Is Less More?," *Science*, 3003:1478-1480, March 5.

Bell, Philip (2003), "Bishop Bell's Brass Behemoths," *Creation*, 25[4]:40-44, September-November.

"Bishop Bell's Dinosaurs" (2007), *Skepticwiki*, June, [On-line], URL: http://skepticwiki.org/index.php/Bishop_Bell's_Dinosaurs.

Bishop, Ellen Morris (1993), "Utah Paleontologist Develops New Look for Sauropod Dinosaurs," *Oregonian*, January 14, [On-line], URL: http://www.bible.ca/tracks/peru-tomb-art.htm.

"Bombardier Beetle" (2007), *Research Machines Encyclopaedia*, [On-line], URL: http://www.tiscali.co.uk/reference/encyclopaedia/hutchinson/m0063590.html.

Boyle, Alan (2007), "Finding a Dinosaur's Soft Spots," *MSNBC*, [On-line], URL: http://cosmiclog.msnbc.msn.com/archive/2007/07/24/288786.aspx.

Butler, Shelley and Deb Kratz (no date), "22 Best Children's Books of 2002," *FamilyFun.com*, [On-line], URL: http://familyfun.go.com/parenting/learn/activities/feature/bestbooks 1202/bestbooks12024.html.

Cabrera, Javier (1975), *El Mensaje de las Piedras Grabadas de Ica* (*The Message of the Engraved Stones of Ica*) (Lima, Peru: INTI-Sol Editores).

Cansdale, G. S. (1996), "Animals of the Bible," *New Bible Dictionary*, ed. J.D. Douglas (Downers Grove, IL: InterVarsity Press), third edition.

Catan, Thomas (2007), "Huge Dinosaur Graveyard Found in Spain," [On-line], URL: http://www.foxnews.com/story/0,2933,313761,00.html.

Cavalli-Sforza, Luigi (2000), *Genes, Peoples, and Languages* (New York: North Point Press).

Cheyne, T.K. (1887), *Job and Solomon* (New York: Thomas Whittaker).

Clayton, John N. (1990), *Dinosaurs—One of God's More Interesting and Useful Creations* (South Bend, IN: John Clayton).

Clayton, John N. (1991), *Does God Exist? Christian Evidences Intermediate Course Teacher's Guide* (South Bend, IN: John Clayton).

Clayton, John (1996), *Does God Exist?*, January/February, [On-line], URL: http://www.doesgodexist.org/JanFeb96/News-Notes.html.

Clayton, John (2007), "What is Reliable History and What is Not," *Does God Exist*, 34[4]:3-7, July/August.

"Coelacanth" (no date), American Museum of Natural History, [On-line], URL: http://www.sciencenews.org/articles/20010505/bob13.asp.

Cohen, Daniel (1975), *The Greatest Monsters in the World* (New York: Dodd, Mead, & Company).

Cooper, Bill (1995), *After the Flood* (Chicester, England: New Wine Press).

Crawford, Maria Luisa (1988), "Sedimentary Rock," *The World Book Encyclopedia* (Chicago, IL: World Book).

Czerkas, Stephen (1992), "New Look for Sauropod Dinosaurs," *Geology*, 20:1068-1070.

Dahmer, Lionel, D. Kouznetsov, et al. (1990), "Report on Chemical Analysis and Further Dating of Dinosaur Bones and Dinosaur Petroglyphs," *Proceedings of the Second International Conference on Creationism*, ed. Robert E. Walsh and Christopher L. Brooks (Pittsburgh, PA: Creation Science Fellowship).

Dawkins, Richard (1986), *The Blind Watchmaker* (New York: W.W. Norton).

Dawson, John William (1895), *The Historical Deluge in Relation to Scientific Discovery* (Chicago, IL: Revell).

De Elvira, M.R. (2007), "Rail Work Points Way to Most Diverse Dinosaur Site in Europe," *Expatica*, [On-line], URL: http://www.expatica.com/actual/article.asp?subchannel_id=81&story_id=46144.

DeYoung, Donald (2000), *Dinosaurs and Creation* (Grand Rapids, MI: Baker).

235

DeYoung, Donald (2005), *Thousands...Not Billions* (Green Forest, AR: Master Books).

"Dig Deeper" (no date), [On-line], URL: http://www.bbc.co.uk/dinosaurs/dig_deeper/finds_ 1.shtml#top.

"Dinosaur Articles 1999" (1999), [On-line], URL: http://www.crystalinks.com/dinosaurs3.html.

"Dinosaur National Monument" (2004), [On-line], URL: http://www.desertusa.com/dino/.

"Dinosaur Reproduction" (2007), [On-line], URL: http://www.enchantedlearning.com/subjects/dinosaurs/anatomy/Repro.shtml.

DiPeso, Charles (1953a), "The Clay Figurines of Acambaro, Guanajuato, Mexico," *American Antiquity*, 18[4]:388-389.

DiPeso, Charles (1953b), "The Clay Monsters of Acambaro," *Archaeology*, Summer, pp. 111-114.

"Diver Finds 'Living Fossil'" (no date), *Science Now*, [On-line], URL: http://www.calacademy.org/science_now/archive/headline_science/coelacanth_010601.php.

Dodson, Peter (1990), "Counting Dinosaurs: How Many Kinds Were There?," *Proceedings of the National Academy of Sciences*, 87:7608-7612, October.

"Dracorex Hogwartsia" (no date), *The Children's Museum of Indianapolis*, [On-line], URL: http://www.childrensmuseum.org/dinosphere/draco_rex/index.html.

"Dragon" (1997), *The New Encyclopedia Britannica*, Micropaedia (Chicago, IL: Encyclopedia Britannica).

Dragons: The Enchanted World (1984), (Alexandria, VA: Time-Life Books).

Dragons: A Fantasy Made Real (2005a), *Animal Planet* (Silver Spring, MD: Discovery Communications).

Dragons: A Fantasy Made Real (2005b), "Trailer: Dragon Culture," *Animal Planet*, [On-line], URL: http://animal.discovery.com/convergence/dragons/dragons.html.

Driver, S.R. and G.B. Gray (1964), *A Critical and Exegetical Commentary on the Book of Job* (Edinburgh: T. & T. Clark).

236

Epp, Theodore H. (1967), *Job, A Man Tried as Gold* (Lincoln, NE: Back to the Bible Publications).

Folklore, Myths and Legends of Britain (1973), (London: Readers' Digest).

"Fossil Evidence" (2007), NOVA, [On-line], URL: http://www.pbs.org/wgbh/nova/id/transitional.html.

Free, Joseph P. and Howard F. Vos (1992), *Archaeology and Bible History* (Grand Rapids, MI: Zondervan).

Freeman, Michael and Claude Jacques (1999), *Ancient Angkor* (Trumbull, CT: Weatherhill).

Funkhouser, J.G. and J.J. Naughton (1968), *Journal of Geophysical Research*, p.4601, July 15.

Gardner, Erle Stanley (1969), *Host With the Big Hat* (New York: William Morrow).

Gebel, Erika (2007), "T. Rex May Be Close Relation to the Chicken," *Charleston Daily Mail*, April 16, [On-line], URL: http://www.dailymail.com/story/Life/2007041620/T-Rex-may-be-close-relation-to-the-chicken/.

"The Geologic Timetable and the Age of the Earth" (2003), Apologetics Press, [On-line], URL: http://www.apologeticspress.org/pdfs/courses_pdf/hsc0304.pdf.

Gibson, Edgar C.S. (1905), *The Book of Job* (London: Methuen).

Good, Edwin (1990), *In Turns of Tempest: A Reading of Job* (Stanford, CA: Stanford University Press).

Gordis, Robert (1965), *The Book of God and Man* (Chicago, IL: University of Chicago Press).

Gordis, Robert (1978), *The Book of Job* (New York: Jewish Theological Seminary of America).

Haines, Tim (1999), *Walking with Dinosaurs: A Natural History* (London: BBC Worldwide).

Hajela, Deepti (2007), "Natural History Museum Show on Dragons," *Associated Press*, May 25, [On-line], URL: http://ca.news.yahoo.com/s/capress/070526/entertainment/art_mythic_creatures.

Hapgood, Charles (1955), *Reports From Acambaro* (New York: Fieldstone School).

Hapgood, Charles (2000), *Mystery in Acambaro* (Kempton, IL: Adventures Unlimited Press).

Harmer, Lowell (1951), "Mexico Finds Give Hint of Lost World: Dinosaur Statues Point to Men Who Lived in Age of Reptiles," *Los Angeles Times*, B1-B2, March 25.

Harrub, Brad and Bert Thompson (2001), "*Archaeopteryx, Archaeoraptor*, and the 'Dinosaurs-to Birds' Theory [Parts I & II]," *Reason & Revelation*, 21[4-5]:25-31,33-39, April-May, [On-line], URL: http://www.apologeticspress.org/articles/473.

Harrub, Brad and Bert Thompson (2003), *The Truth About Human Origins* (Montgomery, AL: Apologetics Press).

Hartley, John E (1988), *The Book of Job* (Grand Rapids, MI: Eerdmans).

Hatcher, Thurston (2002), "Dachshund Survives after Eagle Carries It Off," *CNN*, March 15, [On-line], URL: http://archives.cnn.com/2002/US/03/15/eagle.attack/index.html.

Hayden, Thomas (2002), "A Theory Evolves," *U.S. News & World Report*, 133[4]:42-50, July 29.

Herodotus (no date), *The History of Herodotus*, trans. George Rawlinson, [Online], URL: http://etext.library.adelaide.edu.au/mirror/classics.mit.edu/Herodotus/history.2.ii.html.

Hodge, Bodie (2006), *The New Answers Book* (Green Forest, AR: Master Books).

Hoffman, Emily (2002), "Four Feet Under," *Current Science*, 87[16]: 10-12, May.

Hogarth, Peter and Val Clery (1979), *Dragons* (New York: Viking Press).

Holmes, Stephen (2002), *Life on Earth* (Hauppauge, NY: Barron's Education Series).

Horner, John R. and Don Lessem (1993), *The Complete T. rex: How Stunning New Discoveries are Changing Our Understanding of the World's Most Famous Dinosaur* (New York: Simon & Schuster).

Hoyle, Fred (1960), *The Nature of the Universe* (New York: Harper).

Hu, Yaoming, Jin Meng, Yuanqing Wang, and Chuankui Li (2005), "Large Mesozoic Mammals Fed on Young Dinosaurs," *Nature*, 433:149-152, January 13.

Hubbard, Samuel (1925), *Discoveries Relating to Prehistoric Man by the Doheny Scientific Expedition in the Hava Supai Canyon* (San Francisco, CA: Sunset Press).

Hubbard, Samuel (1926), "African Lions Roamed in Hollywood," *The Dearborn Independent*, 26[35]:12-13,22, June 19.

Jackson, Wayne (1983), *The Book of Job* (Abilene, TX: Quality).

Jacques, Claude and Michael Freeman (1997), *Angkor: Cities and Temples* (Trumbull, CT: Weatherhill).

Jones, Alvin T. (no date), "The American Bison," [On-line], URL: http://www.texasbi son.org/bisonstory.html.

Josephus, Flavius (1987 edition), *The Life and Works of Flavius Josephus: Antiquities of the Jews*, trans. William Whiston (Peabody, MA: Hendrickson).

Keil, C.F. and F. Delitzsch (1996), *Keil and Delitzsch Commentary on the Old Testament* [Electronic Database] (Peabody, MA: Hendrickson).

Kitcher, Philip (1982), *The Case Against Creationism* (Cambridge, MA: MIT Press).

Kramer, Samuel Noah (1959), *History Begins at Sumer* (Garden City, NY: Doubleday).

Krock, Lexi (2003), "Other Fish in the Sea," *NOVA*, January, [On-line], URL: http://www.pbs.org/wgbh/nova/fish/other.html.

Lammerts, Walter, ed. (1971), *Scientific Studies in Special Creation* (Philadelphia, PA: Presbyterian and Reformed).

Lewin, Roger (1990), "Science: Dinosaur Count Reveals Surprisingly Few Species," *New Scientist Archive*, 128[1745], December, [On-line], URL: http://archive.newscientist.com/secure/article/article.jsp?rp=1&id=mg12817452.700.

Lindall, Carl (1996), "Dragon," *World Book Encyclopedia* (Chicago, IL: World Book).

Major, Trevor (1993), "Dating in Archaeology: Radiocarbon & Tree-Ring Dating," Apologetics Press, [On-line], URL: http://www.apologeticspress.org/articles/2019.

Mayor, Adrienne (2005), *Fossil Legends of the First Americans* (Princeton, NJ: Princeton University Press).

McClintock, John and James Strong (1968), *Cyclopaedia of Biblical, Theological and Ecclesiastical Literature* (Grand Rapids, MI: Baker).

McDonald, K.L. and R.H. Gunst, (1967), "Earth's Magnetic Field 1835 to 1965," ESSA Tech. Rept. U.S. Dept. Com.

McLean, Dewey (1995), "The Deccan Trapps Volcanism-Greenhouse Dinosaur Extinction Theory," [On-line], URL: http://filebox.vt.edu/artsci/geology/mclean/Dinosaur_Volcano_Extinction/pages/studentv.html.

Meert, Joseph (2007), "Wild, Wacky World of Answers in Genesis," [On-line], URL: http://scienceantiscience.blogspot.com/2007/01/wild-wacky-world-of-answers-in-genesis.html.

"Meet the Original Cyclops" (no date), *The Classics Pages: Homer's Odyssey*, [On-line], URL: http://www.users.globalnet.co.uk/~loxias/cyclops02.htm.

Meyer, Pedro (2002), "Does the Original Matter?" *WashingtonPost.com*, [On-line], URL: http://media.washingtonpost.com/wp-srv/photo/essays/zonezero/jan_02.htm.

Miller, Dave (2008), "The 'First of the Ways of God,'" Apologetics Press, [On-line], URL: http://www.apologeticspress.org/articles/3627.

Mitchell, T.C. (1996), "Behemoth," *New Bible Dictionary*, ed. J.D. Douglas (Downers Grove, IL: InterVarsity Press), third edition.

Monastersky, Richard (1993), "A Clawed Wonder Unearthed in Mongolia," *Science News*, 143:245, April 17.

Morris, Henry M. (1984), *The Biblical Basis for Modern Science* (Grand Rapids, MI: Baker).

Morris, Henry M. (1988), *The Remarkable Record of Job* (Grand Rapids, MI: Baker).

Morris, Henry M. and John D. Morris (1996), *The Modern Creation Trilogy–Volume 2: Science & Creation* (Green Forest, AR: Master Books).

Morris, John (no date), "Dinosaur Soft Parts," Institute for Creation Research, [On-line], URL: http://www.icr.org/article/2032/.

Norman, David (1991), *Dinosaur!* (New York: Prentice Hall).

Patton, Don (no date), "The Photogallery of the Dinosaur Figurines of Acambaro Mexico," [On-line], URL: http://www.bible.ca/tracks/tracks-acambaro-dinos.htm.

Patton, Don (2006), "Dinosaurs in Ancient Cambodian Temple," [On-line], URL: http://www.bible.ca/tracks/tracks-cambodia.htm.

Payne, J. Barton (1980), *Theological Wordbook of the Old Testament*, ed. R. Laird Harris (Chicago, IL: Moody).

Perkins, Sid (2001), "The Latest Pisces of an Evolutionary Puzzle—Discovery of Coelacanth off Coast of South Africa," *Science News,* May 5, 2001, 159:282, [On-line], URL: http:// www. sciencenews. org/articles/20010505/bob13.asp.

Perkins, Sid (2005), "Old Softy: Tyrannosaurus Fossil Yields Flexible Tissue," *Science News,* 167[13]:195, March 26, [On-line], URL: http://www.sciencenews.org/articles/20050326/fob1.asp.

Perloff, James (1999), *Tornado in a Junkyard: The Relentless Myth of Darwinism* (Arlington, MA: Refuge Books).

Pezzati, Alex (2005), "Mystery at Acambaro, Mexico," *Expedition,* 47[3]:6-7.

Pfeiffer, Charles F. (1960), "Lotan and Leviathan," *Evangelical Quarterly,* 32:208-211.

Polo, Marco (no date), *The Travels of Marco Polo,* [On-line], URL: https://www.nauticus.org/ebooks/TheTravelsofMarcoPoloVolume2.pdf.

Pope, Marvin H. (1965), *Job* (Garden City, NY: Doubleday).

Potter, Ned (2007), "Rediscovering the Dinosaurs," [On-line], URL: http://www.abcnews.go.com/Technology/story?id=3027863&page=1.

Powell, James (1998), *Night Comes to the Cretaceous* (New York: Harcourt Brace & Company).

Pryde, E.B., D.E. Greenway, S. Porter, and I. Roy (1996), *Handbook of British Chronology* (Cambridge: Cambridge University Press), third edition.

Raven, Peter H. and George B. Johnson (1989), *Biology,* (St. Louis, MO: Times Mirror/Mosby College Publishing), second edition.

Reader, John (1981), "Whatever Happened to *Zinjanthropus?*," *New Scientist*, 89:802, March 26.

Rose, Carol (2000), *Giants, Monsters, and Dragons: An Encyclopedia of Folklore, Legend, and Myth* (New York: W.W. Norton).

Ross, Hugh (1998), *The Genesis Question* (Colorado Springs, CO: Navpress).

Rowley, Harold Henry (1980), *Job* (Grand Rapids, MI: Eerdmans).

Russell, William N. (1952), "Did Man Tame the Dinosaur?" *Fate*, 5[2]:20-27.

Sagan, Carl (1977), *The Dragons of Eden* (New York: Random House).

Sanders, Robert (1995), "Pterosaur Insights," [On-line], URL: http://www.berkeley.edu/news/berkeleyan/1995/0503.pterosaur.html.

Schmid, Randolph E. (2006), "New Fossil Overturns Notions of Mammals," *Albuquerque Tribune*, [On-line], URL: http://www.abqtrib.com/albq/nw_science/article/0,2668,ALBQ_21236_4500071,00.html.

Schoch, Robert M. (2003), *Voyages of the Pyramid Builders* (New York: Jeremy P. Parcher/Putnam).

Schweitzer, Mary H., Jennifer L. Wittmeyer, John R. Horner, and Jan K. Toporski (2005), "Soft-Tissue Vessels and Cellular Preservation in Tyrannosaurus rex," *Science*, 307:1952-1955, March 25.

Schweitzer, Mary, et al. (2007), "Analyses of Soft Tissue from Tyrannosaurus rex Suggest the Presence of Protein," *Science*, 316:277-285, April 13.

Shuker, Karl (1995), *Dragons: A Natural History* (New York: Simon & Schuster).

Simpson, George Gaylord, C.S. Pittendrigh and L.H. Tiffany (1957), *Life: An Introduction to Biology* (New York: Harcourt, Brace & Company).

Simpson, Jacqueline (1980), *British Dragons* (London: B.T. Batsford).

Slifer, Dennis (2000), *Guide to Rock Art of the Utah Region* (Santa Fe, NM: Ancient City Press).

Smick, Elmer (1978), "Another Look at the Mythological Elements in the Book of Job," *The Westminster Theological Journal*, 40[2]:213-228, Spring.

Snelling, Andrew (1991), "Where are All the Human Fossils?," *Creation Ex Nihilo*, 14[1]:28-33, December 1991-February 1992.

"The Spread of Dragon Myths" (1981), *Science Digest*, 89:103, May.

"The Stegosaurus Carving that Isn't" (2007), [On-line], URL: http://dinocreationistsfairytale.wordpress.com/2007/01/19/the-stegosaurus-carving-that-isnt/.

Strauss, James D. (1976), *The Shattering of Silence* (Joplin, MO: College Press).

Swift, Dennis (no date[a]), "The Dinosaur Figurines of Acambaro, Mexico," [On-line], URL: http://www.bible.ca/tracks/tracks-acambaro.htm#photo.

Swift, Dennis (no date[b]), *Secrets of the Ica Stones and Nazca Lines* (Dinosaur Institute).

Than, Ker (2007), "Top 10 Beasts and Dragons: How Reality Made Myth," *LiveScience.com*, [On-line], URL: http://www.livescience.com/animals/top10_dragons.html.

Thompson, Bert (2000), *Creation Compromises* (Montgomery, AL: Apologetics Press), second edition.

Thompson, Bert and Brad Bromling, (no date), "Dinosaurs and the Bible," *Apologetics Press Research Article Series* (Montgomery, AL: Apologetics Press).

Tierney, John (1994a), "Coming Soon Near You: A Real Live Jurassic Park," *World Explorer*, 1[4]:15-18.

Tierney, John (1994b), "Pseudoscientific Attacks on Acambaro Artifacts: The Ceramic Technology of Intellectual Suppression," *World Explorer*, 1[4]: 52-61.

Verrengia, Joseph (2005), "Dinosaur Fossils Found in Mammal's Stomach," *LiveScience*, January 12, [On-line], URL: http://www.livescience.com/animals/belly_beast_050112.html.

Watson, Lyall (1982), "The Water People," *Science Digest*, 90[5]:44, May.

243

Weil, Anne (2005), "Living Large in the Cretaceous," *Nature*, 433:116, January 13.

Wharton, James A (1999), *Job* (Louisville, KY: Westminster John Knox).

Whitcomb, John C. (1973), *The World That Perished* (Grand Rapids, MI: Baker).

Whitcomb, John C. and Henry M. Morris (1961), *The Genesis Flood* (Philadelphia, PA: Presbyterian & Reformed).

Wilford, John Noble (2006), "Busy Beaver Swam with Dinosaurs," *Sydney Morning Herald*, [On-line], URL: http://smh.com.au/news/world/busy-beaver-swam-with-dinosaurs/2006/02/24/1140670261970.html.

Wilson, J.V. Kinnier (1975), "A Return to the Problems of Behemoth and Leviathan," *Vetus Testamentum*, 25:1-14, January.

Wolfers, David (1995), *Deep Things Out of Darkness* (Grand Rapids, MI: Eerdmans).

Wysong, R.L. (1976), *The Creation/Evolution Controversy* (East Lansing, MI: Inquiry Press).